VOYAGE
THE TRADE WIND

Photo by Vang Studio

By Harald M. Hamran
John D. Zug, Editor

*Penfield
Press*

Acknowledgments

For their assistance in the preparation of this book, we thank Dr. Marion Nelson, former director of Vesterheim, the Norwegian-American Museum; Darrell Henning, director, Vesterheim; Duane W. Fenstermann, archivist at the Luther College Library, Decorah, Iowa; Betty Seegmiller; Josefa and J. Harry Andersen, Chicago; Joan Liffring-Zug for photography of TradeWind at Vesterheim; Gerald Haas for nautical identification of photographs, and Esther Feske for the cover design.

The TradeWind at Westby Ship Gallery in Vesterheim,
the Norwegian-American Museum in Decorah, Iowa.

Books by Mail, postpaid:
Voyage of the TradeWind (this book) by mail $9.95
Time-Honored Norwegian Recipes Adapted to the American Kitchen $12.95
Notably Norwegian $7.95
Norwegian Recipes: Old-Time Favorites, spiral-bound $5.95
Scandinavian Proverbs $7.95
Stocking Stuffer Series (recipe-card size):
Scandinavian Sweet Treats, spiral-bound, $5.95
Scandinavian Smörgasbord Recipes, spiral-bound, $5.95
Special: *Norwegian Recipes, Scandinavian Sweet Treats,* and *Smörgasbord,* 3 for $16.00
Please send for a complete list of Scandinavian titles available.
Prices subject to change.
Send order to Penfield Press, 215 Brown Street, Iowa City, IA 52245

Contents

Trade wind: a wind that blows toward the equator from the same quarter throughout the year. The general direction is from northeast to southwest on the north side of the equator, and from southeast to northwest on the south side of the equator.
Webster's New Universal Unabridged Dictionary

Vesterheim Membership

You are invited to keep in contact with Vesterheim, the Norwegian-American Museum, through membership. Send for information, or begin your membership by sending $10 (1992 dues for Associate Member) to Vesterheim, 502 West Water Street, Decorah, Iowa 52101. As a member you will receive the Museum's quarterly publication; you will be entitled to free admission to the Museum, and you will receive a 10 percent discount on most purchases from the gift shop, including mail order.

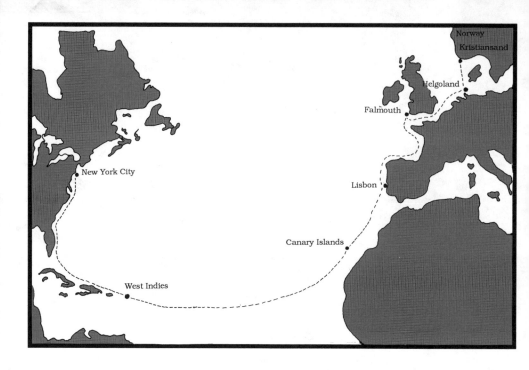

Route of the TradeWind
from Kristiansand, Norway, to New York City

For the Reader

The daily entries in Harald Hamran's logbook, reproduced in this book with permission of Luther College, tell the story of two brothers crossing the Atlantic Ocean in a 25-foot sailboat. The original logbook is document 119:1:2 in the college archives. Hamran wrote in English, and readers may note the following:

N. is for North, W. is for West, S. is for South, and E. is for East. The readings on the compass are in letters, and so are many of the notations in the logbook of "TradeWind." Thus N. N. W. means "North-Northwest," etc.

31-3-33 means March 31, 1933; 1-4-33 means April 1, 1933, etc. Hamran often spelled out the name of the month, and it so appears in this book.

In most cases, Hamran tells distances in miles, but several times the word knot is used. What is a knot? It is one nautical mile an hour (6,080.27 feet or approximately 1.15 miles).

Preface
"Smallest in Recorded History"

It was Sunday, July 30, 1933, and the New York Times dutifully reported: "125 days out of Kristiansand, Norway, the TradeWind, a 25-footer, sailed into New York Harbor yesterday and docked at Sixty-ninth Street, Brooklyn. Her crew comprised two brothers, Harald and Hans Hamran. . . .

"Bronzed and bearded after weeks at sea, the brothers saw nothing unusual in the accomplishment of their 8,302-mile trip.

"'It was lots of fun,' they declared.

"Thousands came to see the little boat in New York. The welcome included a parade on Broadway and greetings by the mayor."

Never in recorded history had anyone sought to cross the Atlantic in a smaller boat.

Today, the brothers are sailors in the sky, but their "little TradeWind" retains its magic as an ever-popular exhibit at Vesterheim, the Norwegian-American Museum in Decorah, Iowa. After arriving to see the Chicago World's Fair, the brothers sold their boat to Arthur Andersen, founder of the accounting firm that bears his name. In 1934, Andersen shipped the boat to Decorah by rail as a gift to Luther College, the Museum's founding institution.

"Little?" The boat is so big that Luther employee Carl Nickoley and his sons Frank and Arthur had to tear down a brick wall, pull the boat inside on rollers, and re-lay the brick. Even then, the room was not high enough, and for many years the mast and sails remained horizontal on the deck of the ship.

In 1975, the room was replaced by a three-story addition, the Museum's Westby Ship Gallery, and ever since, the TradeWind's mast and sails have proudly reached upward to their highest. Today the TradeWind is the centerpiece of the Gallery, and "The Atlantic Crossing" is one of the most popular attractions of the Museum.

> —*Darrell Henning, Director, Vesterheim*
> *The Norwegian-American Museum*

Thousands have visited the Westby Ship Gallery to see the 25-foot boat which the Hamran brothers sailed across the Atlantic in 1933.

The Spirit of Adventure

Harald Hamran   Hans Hamran

I have always been an adventurer. My fifteenth birthday was spent in a sealer in the Arctic Ocean. After that (in 1911) I went to sea, and ran away from an English ship in Australia in 1913. In that country I was a hobo, a gold digger (in Kalgoorlie), a hunter, and a sailor, until I left there in October 1919.

On my wanderings I have been to lots of strange and also famous places. I have gone on foot across Berthoud Pass in the Rockies of Colorado in the middle of March (1920), have trapped in northern Ontario (1920-21), have fished on the coast of British Columbia (1925), and have been in London, Paris, and New York.

Such a nature as mine finds no peace, no satisfaction in a soft, comfortable life or in watching the clock—plugging away on a regular job. It does not seem real life to me. Far better to take chances with storm and difficulties even if life itself must be staked.

I have always admired ships and boats. Even now I can stand for hours and enjoy the lines—the rigging—of a fine vessel, and go back day after day to the same place and do the same. A fine ship really lights my eye.

I had been in an oil tanker that ran between the East Indies, China, and Australia, occasionally getting as far west as the Red Sea, when I was discharged in Suez in September, 1932. After

7

spending three weeks in Egypt I left for Oslo, Norway, where I met my brother Hans, who I had not seen since 1911. That is 21 years. He had run away from home when he was 14 to go to sea and had also become a "man without a country."

We decided to be partners in a venture to cross the Atlantic Ocean in a 25-foot boat, with sail only. We decided to name the boat "TradeWind," maybe a common but as far as we knew an original ship's name. And to us a name with sun and sea breeze and starry nights and green islands inside the horizon.

We helped to build the boat, planed the boards, did the riveting and nailing, sewed the sails, and rigged it up the way we thought best. We laid in a low deck and under this we kept the provisions. We had a Bermuda rig, but the mast was comparatively low—23 feet. The boat was nine feet wide.

The boat was finished at the end of February and, after trying it out under sail on the fjord (Flekkefjord) for a couple of days, we tied up at the wharf and had a host of curious visitors aboard. And the most interesting of the people who came aboard was white-haired, smiling, ever-cheerful Lars Hansen, the author. The first time he visited us he wished himself twenty years younger so he could make the trip with us. The second time he came at dinnertime in a snowstorm. We were just in the act of frying some herring and had boiled some potatoes. As we had scarcity of space in our little cabin, he tucked himself away in a bunk and talked of the Arctic and the men he had known up there in the "old days." Now and then he took a boiled potato out of the dish and peeled and ate it. (4-3-1933).

He gave us a copy of his last book *Björnar Balk og hans slekt* (Björnar Balk and His Family), and spoke of a book he was then writing and had nearly finished, which he was going to name *Frelsen og naadin* (Salvation and Mercy). A person like him (L.H.) is always interesting.

We were ready to start our voyage and had gotten our unpleasant experience on a farm at a distance when we were hiking and the farmer would not sell us a cup of coffee. On such a farm, in my opinion, there was very little hospitality.

We had a cozy, comfortable life aboard the "TradeWind." The coffee pot was almost at all times warm, slices of salt pork sizzled in the frying pan at breakfast every morning, and flapjacks (American style) were made by the hundreds.

Friday the tenth of March 1933 we were towed out (it was dead calm) to Anabel Island, about eight miles, and as a breeze from southeast was blowing we stood (sailed) out Flekkefjord past Värnes Lighthouse and at 7:30 in the evening we had Lister light abeam, distant about 6 miles. At nine o'clock a thick fog came and as we did not wish to be caught near shore in the regular coastwise ship channels, at 11:30 we stood (sailed) south about 28 miles. We were outbound at 2 o'clock Saturday morning and came up to the coast about 10 miles west of Lindesnes. All Saturday 11-3-33 was foggy and a dead calm lasted till Sunday morning when a light breeze rose from the west which took us on Sunday around the southernmost point of Norway—Lindesnes.

In connection with this period of our voyage I always remember a couple of amusing incidents. We were lying outside Lister Lighthouse when a couple of large ships were approaching us— one from East, one from West. Both ships were very near to us. We could plainly hear the churn of the propellers, talk, and whistling. We didn't have any foghorn aboard the "TradeWind" and some kind of signal was needed to make our presence known.

So I grabbed a bucket and a marlin spike and Hans (he was making flapjacks) flung a flapjack out of the pan onto a plate on my bunk, got hold of a planer, and started battering the frying pan. The effect was terrible. I guess some old pilot cursed the fog that night and cursed the unearthly noise from our fog-signal instruments.

The next morning I was trying to get our bearings by the fog siren when I thought I heard a ship very near to us. I listened very hard and heard—I thought—the regular noise of the waves breaking from her bow. I listened longer and decided it was a diesel-motor vessel and walked forward to hear better because the mainsail was slamming and making a noise. I came around the companionway and stopped dead. The frightfulest, loudest, and most unearthly snoring that I ever heard had fooled me. Hans was snoring and that boy could sure snore!

9

The night Sunday-Monday was calm. A strong current set us westward and a thick fog came on so at 6:30 on Monday morning we took bearings of the Lindesnes fog siren and its position was north. A breeze, light but freshening when the sun came up, gave us favorable wind past Ryvingen Songvår to Flekkerø and into Kristiansand, where we arrived Monday 5:30 p.m. 13-3-33.

Tuesday the fourteenth (14-3) we were visited by a photographer from *Norsk Telegraph* bureau, who took pictures of us and our little vessel. In the afternoon we were rung up on the telephone by *Tidens Tegn* and in the evening by *Aftenposten*. Earlier in the day we were interviewed by a journalist from *Fædrelands Vennen,* which paper in the afternoon had a very interesting article about us. A butter factory (Johnsens) sent down 24 pounds of butter. Visitors, a host of them, were on the quay all day, discussing us and viewing us.

Wednesday March 15 here in Kristiansand it was rainy and the snow was one meter high in the streets. The snow is melting this morning. We went to the custom house and made arrangement with inspector V. D. Lippe to measure our "TradeWind" in the morning so we would be able to take out provisions free of duty. Curious visitors, again a host of them, were all day on the quayside, looking us over and giving us all sorts of advice.

Our flapjack-makings (batter) is getting all over our ship. But never mind: It is wonderful to be alive and kicking and eating flaps.

16-3-33. Kristiansand. A couple of drugstores sent us an assortment of drugs and medicines and a dealer in ropes and canvas sent us an assortment of his wares. People are very much interested in us and our voyage. I believe there is still adventurous blood here in this town—a heritage from the old sailing-ship days when this was one of the largest shipping towns in Norway.

At eight o'clock this morning came two men from the customs house and one from the harbor office to take measurements of our little boat. While doing this they joked about the job as it was the smallest vessel they had ever been called on to measure. And no wonder. Our little "TradeWind" is only 3 1/2 tons.

17-3-33. Today we laid down dunnage and made a bulkhead in the afterpart of the ship. We had a visit of an old-timer who just after the war sailed a small pilot cutter from here (Kristiansand) to Port Natal in South Africa. A ship chandler sent us some oakum (for calking) in case we'd need it on the trip.

Tidens Tegn, one of the largest papers in Norway, came out with a long article about us and also had a very good picture of our boat. It has been raining all day, yet a never-ending stream of curious visitors has been coming and going all the time. They are all wondering at our daring, yet I believe it is an ordinary thing but strange or uncommon because it is not tried too often.

I cannot but mention the women. They are admiring us. There is not the slightest doubt about that. I am tempted to wish myself ten years younger.

18-3-1933. Another drugstore sent us an assortment of medicines. We certainly have enough pills and powders to take us across the Atlantic Ocean. If we only knew how to use it all, but doctors (physicians) do not seem to have taken into consideration our ignorance about medicine. All the same they have been hospitable and liberal toward us and we are certainly obliged to them and to a host of others who have shown an unusual interest in us. Customs inspector V. D. Lippe came personally aboard today and delivered a measurement certificate of our boat. It is the smallest boat ever measured in Kristiansand, but what of that! It is seaworthy and it is ours.

Sun. 19-3-1933. Northwest and snow. Yet hundreds of people—a never-ending stream of people—have been coming and going here to see us. Business people, Americans on visit here, people from Nordland where we come from, sailors of all descriptions, and girls. We are almost worn out talking to our visitors. Some of them—the ones who don't know the sea and Father Neptune's tricks, suggest safety devices of all descriptions. If we should put their safety devices into use, our "TradeWind" would be so overloaded she would sink right here alongside the wharf.

A student wants to be with us; also a sea captain. Another

man who has been in Alaska for years has asked us more than once if we'd take him as a partner in the venture. But we cannot as all our plans and outfit would have to be altered.

20-3-33. Lars sewed tarpaulins all day. Was interviewed by a journalist from *Kristiansand Tidende* and by a correspondent for *Sunmøreposten*. The usual crowd of visitors—captains and millionaires, bums and girls.

21-3-33. The last of the sail sewing was done today and finished for a while until old Father Neptune takes his anger full on our sails. *Kristiansand Tidende* came out with a long article about us, 2 1/2 columns. The long-waited-for letter from Eldis (home) arrived today. As far as can be gathered, our proposed trip is creating a sensation at home. We had an offer of more medicine but we have sufficient of that commodity. More than enough. Weather cold and clear. If we had been ready we would have made a start on our voyage.

22-3-33. We made a binnacle for the compass—fastened the watertight bag in the cockpit and strengthened the boom with a couple oak strips today. Had a visit of an artist (one of the gentle sex) who had taken pictures of us and our little vessel. She is very good-looking and her name is Johanne (Tulla) Kleffel, King St. 9, Kristiansand S. We have this last few days been bothered by a queer visitor. He is always half-drunk and he is at all hours reciting the mother's speech by the grave, from *Peer Gynt*. I am sick and tired of it. Occasionally he wants to borrow money. I believe he is a missionary who strayed from the narrow path. Poor devil—if only he'd keep quiet for awhile. S. Gerrard, a big merchant, sent us down some stores (provisions).

23-3-33. Sent down today as a gift was a case of milk from the Norwegian milk factories (Viking Milk Company), also four cases of canned meats, salt pork, salt meat, from Stumpf, the largest butcher in town. People are very hospitable and take an unusual interest in "TradeWind," her voyage, and her crew consisting of two brothers. Our artist friend (Johanne Kleffel) was again today on a visit aboard and also invited us home at 6 o'clock tonight *(Styhe)*.

Also had lots of people on visit today. But mostly girls today. Schoolteachers take their pupils from the classrooms to the wharf (quay) to view us.

Lovely weather. Maybe spring is just around the corner. It is wonderful to have good health, to be alive, to be courting danger, to be free, and to have adventure.

24-3-33. Today has been a lovely day. Sunshine and spring. Lots of visitors. A packet of books and reading matter was sent aboard. Also a few other small presents. Shifted this morning to the railroad wharf and took aboard 900 pounds of sand-ballast in bags. Put safety lines on the rudder, also a safety strap. We also did a few things that had to be done—overlooked and served the forestay, made sharepoles, and stowed away provisions. The ship is ready for her voyage.

25-3-33. Ship's biscuits and all kinds of "hardtack" were sent us from a bread factory (Gammillo Bastrup) and other small gifts from people, among other things a Bible. Well, we may need it. Who knows? People have been wonderful here in town. They have taken an abnormal interest in us. A sea anchor and cable came down as a gift from a big merchant, S. Gerrard. He is interested in the sea and sailors. All provisions are aboard—provisions and water for 2-3 months. Good-bye Kristiansand, good-bye Norway, and good-bye Eldis. We are bound for the sea.

Sunday 26 March 1933. A lovely day—sunshine and spring, green pine trees on the hills and among the green pine trees the silver-white trunks of the birches which are getting the peculiar green tint just before the leaves spring out. Hundreds of people on the wharf, and on the roads leading to town are other hundreds who are viewing us. Kristiansand—we have only fond memories of you. Lots of people have their cameras with them and are taking pictures of us. This morning after looking over the weather reports and finding these favorable, we hoisted sail and for a very light breeze from W.S.W. we got out of Kristiansand harbor. Outside the harbor a dead calm prevailed, so at 8 o'clock we tied up in a little bay just outside the town.

Monday 27-3-33. At ten o'clock a fresh breeze from W.S.W. rose and we hoisted sail and stood out from Odderøen. At 11:10 we had Oksø Lighthouse abeam and steering by the wind a course of S. by W. 1/2 W. At one o'clock we lost sight of old Norway. We had Oksø light north—distant about 12 miles. Speed about 6 miles.

Land of the Vikings, shall we ever see you again? Many fond memories will ever be with us from this country. As we were on our way out today we passed a lot of fishing smacks and the pilots were all cheering us—waving their caps and wishing us "bon voyage." *Kristiansand Tidende* had an article yesterday about us leaving. Never mind! We are on our voyage today. At 4 o'clock in the afternoon the wind turned more westerly and we altered the course to S.W. by S. 1/2 S. At 8:15 we had Hanstholm Lighthouse 4 points on our port bow and at 11 o'clock abeam and distant about 16 miles. We are steering from 10 o'clock S.W. 1/2 S. with close-hauled sheets by the wind so we can by a very narrow margin go clear the banks—shallows and reefs of Jutland. Hope the weather holds till we get clear of the reefs. Visibility good.   H. H.

Cheek Block

Will We Ever Make England?

Tuesday 28-3-33. Breezes fresh W.S.W., choppy sea. At 5:30 in the morning we had Thybb Røn light abeam. Close in on the reefs. 11 a.m. Bovbjerg light abeam, distant 6 miles. Wind and sea as above. Course S.W. 1/2 S. Hope we can stand clear of Horn Reef on this tack.

Cooking is impossible—even for such an ordinary everyday thing as coffee—without a hand on the kettle handle till the water boils. But we have biscuits and bacon and raw vegetables—and in spite of all, life is wonderful. From 3 o'clock to 4 in the afternoon the wind died down gradually so "TradeWind" had hardly enough speed to steer. At six o'clock p.m. a gentle breeze from west stiffened the sail bunting and gave her a speed of about 4 miles. Course S.W. & W. Leeway 1/2 p.m. Course S.W. 10 p.m. Rinkøling beacon E.N.E., distant 15 miles.

Wednesday 29-3-1933. 12 midnight to 7 a.m. S.W. speed 4 miles. Calm sea. A wonderful morning, a gentle breeze, hardly enough to stiffen the sails. We are on the northwestern edge of Horn Reef and can hear the fog siren in the south. This morning we got in among the Danish fishing fleet. Our little "TradeWind" with her new canvas and her name in big black letters painted on her mainsail is no doubt a curiosity here. Several fishing smacks have come fairly near to take a look at us. One of them, "Norma" of Esbjerg, came within a couple cable lengths and stopped her engine. I steered alongside her and after having a chat, one of her crew threw on our deck a big bucketful of lales (red-spotted flounders). They shall taste well for dinner today. Three cheers for the Esbjerg fishing smack "Norma." At 11 a.m. our course was west. Speed about 2 miles. 2 p.m. Current getting strongly N.E. "Horn Reef" Lightship visible direct S.W. At 9 p.m. course South and passed over the shallows on Horn Reef at 11 p.m. The seas were topping in pyramid forms. Sea birds screeching. The rumble of the breakers sounded like a distant cannonade. Depth where we crossed the reef 3 1/6 fathoms. Cold, starlight, clear. Visibility good.

Thursday 30-3-33. Course S.E. to 6 a.m. beating up under the S.W. lightship. Strong current setting N.N.E. Choppy sea. Wind unsteady from south. Our usual flapjacks and bacon for breakfast. They sure taste good with 2-3 cups of strong coffee after 5-6 hours in the cockpit. This is real life. We are in among the Danish fishing fleet. Now and then a fishing cutter comes alongside our little "TradeWind" to chat with us, asking us where we are bound, and showing surprise when we tell them we are bound for the U.S.A.

The redspots yesterday were a treat. At 10 in the morning we put the vessel on the starboard tack for a S.W. breeze that during the afternoon turned gradually more westerly. We steered a course of S.S.E. following the wind gradually coming up to S.W. by S. At 11 p.m. we were under Rode Kliff light.

31 March 1933. At 2 a.m. our course was S.S.W. Fresh breeze. Visibility no good. 6 a.m. Hornum Point Light abeam. 8 a.m. Amrum Light abeam distant 8 miles. Current setting west at the rate of 8-10 miles. Breeze W.S.W. very fresh. Choppy bad sea. Shallow water. Hope we will get across the shallows and submerged reefs without knocking our little "TradeWind" to pieces.

11 a.m. Across the reef (Holt Knob). Where we passed Holt Knob only 1 1/2 fathoms in water. When we passed the reefs, Hans was sitting in the cabin playing mandolin, quite unconcerned. At 12 noon small storm from west. Got up to Anssne-Eide Lightship at 3:15 p.m. Beating up west under Helgoland N.W. and S.W. under shortened sail.

1 April 1933. We were beating up west under Helgoland and arrived there at 7 o'clock a.m., tying up at the excursion pier at 7:30. It's raining. Outside is a very heavy sea from west—and as the wind also is W.by S. we decided to seek shelter here. It's not much use battling against wind and sea when it's head-on.

Helgoland looks magnificent from the sea and especially so seen from south, north, and west. Although it is raining hard the pier is full of curious onlookers.

10 p.m. in Helgoland harbor. This place reminds me of the world war and the age of the kaisers. Iron and cement battlements, railroads, and tunnels through the rock—such is Helgoland, but the claws of all this are cut. The big guns are dismounted.

The night is chilly and clear. A fresh wind from W.N.W. is blowing. Just above us Helgoland Lighthouse is flashing its enormous beam of light, one of the strongest in the world. On a clear night when visibility is good, the light can be seen at Brunsbuttel, a distance of 47 miles. All is well.

Sunday 2 April 1933. Fine weather and lots of visitors, but the wind is blowing continually from west—head on. In the harbor we are the only ship flying the Norwegian flag. We are having a good time—eating, sleeping, talking, and writing. A lot of real lovely girls are stopping on the pier to look us over.

We have invitations to come aboard the Danish Bethelship, also an invitation from a German businessman for tonight. Had a long walk around the island today. It is a gigantic work that is laid down on this island—concrete, tunnels, gaping holes in cliff walls where once there were guns, and wrecks of barb wire and other means of defense. On a red rocky pillar, isolated from the island by a narrow channel—deep, but only a couple or three fathoms of water—stands an Iron Cross.

But other times have come—*sic transit gloria mundi.* H. H.

Monday 3 April 33. Westerly winds—squalls and heavy seas. So we may as well make ourselves cozy and comfortable in Helgoland harbor. Some Danish fishermen gave us a few large codfish and 44 redspots (flounders) about 10-12 inches long. The Danes have shown themselves as real comrades. I shall not forget their friendliness and sympathy. Denmark and Danes! You are showing yourselves as a friendly neighborly people. We in Norway are often not that way.

This afternoon we had tea with a businessman who has traveled a good deal in Norway. His name is August Kuchlurz. Very pleasant people. His only daughter is a beautiful female wonder. She was chosen to present Field Marshal August von

Mackensen a bouquet of roses on his last visit to Helgoland. She is an angel.

Tuesday 4 April 1933. Today is a day of "in memoriam" to me. Martha Nelson and the 4th of April. The weather seems to be calming down. The harbor master was aboard asking for and looking over our papers. Hope we can soon get on our way. Helgoland is very pleasant, but we have a long voyage before us. Wind and sea are still head-on. There are a lot of Danish fishing cutters laying in Helgoland harbor because of the bad weather. They are very friendly—often on visit and curious to hear the result of the finding in the Greenland question.

Good luck Danes! I wish you all good things. You are a friendly, comradely, hospitable people.

Wednesday 5 April 1933. Weather fine with a fresh breeze from N.W. A Danish fishing cutter "Este" offered to tow us out of the harbor and at 7:15 a.m. we started out from our snug shelter. At 8 a.m. they let us loose and we hoisted sail and stood for a rather weak N.W. breeze a course of W. Later in the day the wind calmed down and turned more W. so we had to fall off gradually to W.S.W.

Thursday 6 April. Weak wind from W. At 2 a.m. we had "Nordering" Lightship in sight and at 3:45 abeam. Course N.W. At 8 a.m. we were making a course of S.W. Visibility poor, speed about 3 miles. At about 8 o'clock in the evening it started to blow rather fresh from the north. We held a westerly course and had Borkum light abeam at 11 p.m. Speed 7 miles. Visibility good.

Friday 7 April 1933. Wind fresh N. At 3:30 in the morning we passed "Borkum Reef" Lightship and at 8 we had Ameland light abeam course W. Lots of ships and strong breeze. About noon the breeze died down and we laid the rest of the day in a dead calm and drifted with the tides and listened to the sails slamming. The "Kap Polonis" passed us outward bound and the "President Roosevelt" passed us a cable length away. The rails were lined with her passengers and crew looking us over. A

French ship from Boulogne, going east, came up to us and asked where we were bound. We certainly look a little out of the ordinary wherever we go.

I shall not forget our sailing last night. The wind was fresh and abeam and a bright moon shone. Our "TradeWind" seemed to almost lift herself from the sea and just skimmed the waves, leaving a snowy wake of foam astern. I believe it was a swan— anyway it was a large, long-necked white bird—that must have been sleeping and was run over by us. I was steering and was startled to hear the screeching of this bird as it flapped away from the boat. And it seemed to have come right out of the side of the boat.

Yes, all things and everybody is all right. Reading, sleeping, thinking, eating and laying plans for the future—dreaming. What is life without dreams? We are drifting outside Terchelling light. But what of that? There will be enough of wind before we get to Uncle Sam and New York.

Saturday 8 April 1933. We have laid in a dead calm outside these Frisian Islands all day—between Terchelling light and the lightship of the same name. Swarms of migrating birds are on their way north. At times they are all over the "Tradewind." Tired after their long journey, no doubt. I can see them shut their eyes and draw themselves together as soon as they get on our deck or in our rigging. For several days, lots of wild geese have been flying north.

This morning the "Balzac" of Oslo came alongside and without stopping exchanged a few words. They promised to report us. The sun set in a riot of colors—gold, violet, red, copper, and a blue sea hid at last the golden ball from view.

God, it's glorious to live!

Sunday 9 April 1933. A gentle breeze from S.W. As usual head-on from 12-8 a.m. We steered W.S.W. At 8 we laid her on the other tack for a course of S.S.W. The breeze freshened about noon and laying a course of S.S.W. for close-hauled sheets and making a speed of about 6 knots, we made "Haade" Lightship outside the mouth of Texrel at 11 p.m.

Monday 10 April. In a dead calm east of the mouth of the Feadle with the "Haade" Lightship in E.N.E. Distance 8 miles. 12 noon, sound 13 fathoms. Strong current. The porpoises are playing around the "TradeWind" occasionally touching the boat with their fins. In the evening around 6 p.m. a light breeze from S.S.W. came, giving us a speed of 1.4 miles. We kept a course of W.S.W. throughout the night.

A full moon was in view but visibility was poor on account of a light haze that lasted till sunrise.

Tuesday 11 April 1933. All day we have had an even breeze from S.S.W. We have steered a course of W. by S. and W.S.W. We are heading for the Yarmouth banks—"Merrie England."

This morning an English trawler, the "Tower" of Grimsby— Skipper Fielding—hailed us and asked "Ow we'd like a bit of fish." We said "Thank you" of course and came alongside him. He presented us with some nice flounders, some English chewing tobacco, some fresh newspapers, and a "cup o' tay" (cup of tea). Here we heard of the terrible American airship disaster. They were very pleasant and hospitable on the "Tower." We autographed the skipper's logbook and he shook hands with us and said with real friendliness, "I hope you will get there, boys."

Apropos tobacco! We are rather hard on it these chilly nights, and with regard to airships: I would rather be on this little nutshell of a boat than up there in the skies. I am not forgetting that this little nutshell may be the means of me getting up in the skies. But water seems more akin to "terra firma" than air.

Wednesday 12 April 1933. A light breeze from N.W. carried us from about 10 miles west of Smiths Knoll with a speed of around 4 miles to here near the "Outer Gabbard" Lightship. It died out, however, between 11 a.m. and 12 noon, leaving us on a sea as calm and unruffled as a sheet of glass. Well, it's good to start observing patience. This is like old sailing-ship days— depending on weather and wind.

We had some of Stumpf's sausages for dinner today. They are very good and tasty. In the evening around 9 o'clock the weather got foggy and the sky in the north was black. Under this a sea full of phosphorescence looked like a myriad of lights when the waves broke. Around 9 p.m. a rather fresh wind from North rose and a strong current was setting us westward. "Outer Gabbard" lightship about 10 p.m. Course S-W. Wind N. Speed 6 miles.

Thursday 13 April 1933. The day began with squally weather and a fresh wind from N.N.E. "I Nord Hinder" Lightship abeam at 5:30 a.m. "II West Hinder" Lightship abeam at 9 a.m. Speed about 6 miles. Through the forenoon the haze lifted and visibility became very good. At 12 o'clock noon we passed Ostende (Belgium) in a fine Northeaster.

How pleasant it feels to have favorable wind. If it would only last. The wind turned easterly as the day went by and at times it was rather fresh. At 7:30 p.m. we had Dunkerque abeam. At 9 we saw the magnificent light at Cape Crisnes. At 11:30 p.m. we were abreast of Calais.

Friday 14 April 1933. From midnight a strong current setting eastward became felt—gradually growing stronger. It was so strong that it set us across the straits North of the South Toreland light by 3 a.m., a distance of about 20 miles.

It shifted, however, between 5-6 a.m. The wind was still easterly but weak. At 9 a.m. we had Dover abeam; at 10:30 we had Folkestone abeam; at 1 p.m. we had Dungeness light abeam distant about 1 1/2 miles. The weather fine—sunshine and a smooth sea.

Ships are altering their course to steer nearby us—to look us over, no doubt. We are an unusual craft in these parts. We are flying the Norwegian flag at the masthead.

At 6:15 p.m. we had the "Royal Sovereign" Lightship astern and at 8 o'clock p.m. we were abreast of Beachy Head.

During the day, a ship from Kristiansand, the "Aguila," hailed us and wished us good voyage. England is a beautiful country and at its best on a day like this. The sun shining warm, cloudless skies, a day in spring, a blue channel, a breeze from the east. Up from this blue sea rise the white cliffs, so peculiar for this part of the country, and on top of the cliffs stretch gently sloping and level green fields broken only by a little holt of trees here and there. Beautiful sun! Beautiful world!

Saturday 15 April 1933. By midnight the wind died down to an occasional unsteady gust from S.W. that now and then filled the sails.

At 8:30 a.m. we passed the "Owers" Lightship. But later in the forenoon the tide set us back to 5-6 miles eastward of it. Between 12 noon and 1 p.m. a fresh breeze rose from the southwest and the tide being with us from 3 p.m. we passed the lightship the second time at 4:15 p.m. Strong current and a very choppy bad sea. We could only lay W.N.W. so we decided to make for the sound between the mainland and the Isle of Wight and accordingly altered our course at 6:15 p.m. to N.W.

My partner is always having trouble with the primus-apparat in his capacity as cook on his cooking days.

Some bad language is sure to issue from the cabin and occasionally a thick smoke fills our living quarters when a pot has capsized or the primus has taken a playful turn and lays bottom up or races around smoking. Cooking aboard the "TradeWind" is an art as difficult to learn as juggling aboard here. They amount to the same thing. Cooking is juggling.

At 7 p.m. we steered past the fortifications (outer) in Portsmouth Sound and tied up at a little wharf in a little summer resort town by the name of Seaview on the Isle of Wight. The time was then 8:15 p.m. It is going to be a night's peaceful sleep in port for once in a blue moon.   H.H.

Sunday 16 April 1933. A fine day, but dead calm. After going ashore for some newspapers and a drink of English ale we cast loose and drifted with the tide west. All day passed without any wind and by midnight we were by the southeast corner of the Island (Isle of Wight).   Seaview 16-4-33

Monday 17 April 1933. At 4 a.m. a fresh wind started blowing from the east, getting fresher as the day wore on. We were forging ahead on a course of west doing about 8 miles. At 10 a.m. we reefed our mainsail and took in the jib. It slackened the speed some, but it was necessary—safety first. In the afternoon around 6 p.m. the wind moderated a little. It was still fresh, however, and heavy sea was running. At 6:15 p.m. we sighted Start Point and set our course for Torquay, where we arrived at 11:45 p.m.

Torquay 17-4-33

Tuesday 18 April 1933. Weather fresh easterly so it is hard to get clear of the shallows if we try to go clear Start Point. We may as well lay in port. Had a visit aboard of a captain of a racing yacht. The customs were also aboard. We are moored to a buoy in the inner harbor. In the afternoon (5 p.m.) we went alongside and bought a supply of potatoes and vegetables and also filled our casks with fresh water. Torquay is a lovely town with wide, clean streets, fine houses, and nice people. But then it is also called "The English Riviera." A myriad of lights of all colors bedecks the waterfront, giving it an Oriental touch.

Wednesday 19 April 1933. Sunshine and clear with a fresh wind from the east. At 9 a.m. we left our snug berth at buoy 14 and set sail for Falmouth. At 1:30 p.m. we had Start Point abeam (N). Steering a course of W. At 6 p.m. sighted Eddystone light in N.W. Wind moderating some but still a fresh east breeze. Rigged the jib out as a tri-sail abeam, using the handle of a boat-hook as a yard. This is sure life. I would not change places with King George. A boat our own. The kingdom of the sea ours—no laws, no taxes, no competition with other fellow-beings. Just God, and nature, and ourselves.

At 8 p.m. we had Eddystone light abeam distant about 9 miles. At 10 p.m. we sighted the Lizard light. Wind fresh but even.

Thursday 20 April 1933. Wind fresh from east with squalls. Reefed the mainsail and took the jib off her at 2 a.m. Lizard light W.N.W. Course N.W. Arrived in Falmouth at 3:30 a.m.

We steered her into Falmouth in the dead of night and neither I nor my partner had any knowledge of the port. After cruising all around the harbor looking for a snug place to moor our "TradeWind" we tired of it and made fast at the stern of a scow.

We certainly did some sailing last night. She must have made between 8-9 miles before we reefed her down. She left a wake of foam astern and in the center a streak of light caused by the phosphorescence in the water.

Writing and posting mail today.

Friday 21 April 1933. In the harbor of Falmouth. Writing and making preparations before crossing the Bay of Biscay. Letters arrived from Lars Hansen and from friends in Kristiansand S.

Was interviewed by some reporters, and press photographers were taking an incredible number of pictures of us and our little vessel.

Was ashore shopping and got some fresh meat and other small delicacies dear to the heart of a sailor. Harald Hamran.

Saturday 22 April 1933. A lovely day—sunshine and warm and the harbor like a sheet of glass. Did some alterations on the sails and had visitors of all sorts aboard. As we are laying on the stream (in the current) they have to borrow rowboats to come and see us but that does not deter our visiting, curious English friends.

The *Plymouth Morning News* came out with pictures of us and our boat and also had an article about us.

The weather changed this afternoon. Cloudy and southwest wind. This clear sky and eastern weather has lasted for almost two weeks now. Pity it did not continue for another week. It would have carried us across the Bay of Biscay.

Sunday 23 April 1933. In the harbor of Falmouth. A S.W. wind is blowing and occasionally it is raining. Today has been a peaceful day and we have enjoyed it, but we would rather have been on our way.

It is cozy and comfortable in our little cabin. When we are tired of talking and writing we do some reading, for there are a lot of books and periodicals aboard. The trouble is to keep them dry. We have already thrown overboard not a small amount of reading stuff that had become wet and seemed hopeless to again be gotten in a condition to be read. But never mind! We are not here to read but to cross the Atlantic Ocean in a 25-foot boat.

Falmouth 23-4-33 H. M. Hamran

Monday 24 April 1933. S.W. wind and rain. Both of us have been aboard all day reading, writing, eating, and sleeping. A gray mist is covering the hillsides and town, and it gives one a depressed feeling to look outside, so we are like an ostrich that sticks its head in the sand. Then we shut the door to keep out the rain and fog, and brew us a good cup of tea and get hold of a good book. Good humor must be had at all costs.

Tuesday 25 April 1933. The fog cleared off this morning, giving us an occasional glimpse of the sun. But a fresh south-wester is still blowing so it is not much use leaving our snug berth with wind and sea head-on.

Had a telegram this morning from some unknown person who wants to be with us. "Wish to accompany. Wire what money required. Rennie. Post Restante Rutherglen." Well, we have had others who wanted the same thing, but must refuse as we have no room and space.

It is a pity we cannot get favorable wind so we could be on our way. But everything has its day. So also with the wind. It will come from the right direction some day and blow us across the dreaded Bay of Biscay.

Wednesday 26 April 1933. Wind and sun, and the wind going more westerly. Oh, if only it would last for a few days so we could make a start. The English papers all have pictures of us and some of them have articles.

In the afternoon it began to rain very heavy, so we have been in our cabin all day, reading. There is a notice in the Sunday pictorial about an Austrian couple who are on a trip similar to ours. They also are trying to cross the "Pond," but their boat is only 23 feet long and has a beam of 4 feet (?). I cannot see any chance of success in their venture, unless they are exceptionally fortunate. Of course I ought not speak so loud; ours is not much better. They have the advantage of starting from Lisbon while we have also to battle with the North Sea and the Bay of Biscay.

Thursday 27 April 1933. Had some visitors (of the better class) aboard today. They came in motor launches and there was no help for us; we had to pose for pictures again. I am beginning to hate cameras.

Wind varying from W. to N.W. Cloudy. At 6:56 p.m. we beached the boat in town on a fine sandy beach and scrubbed the bottom and painted it. All evening a host of visitors were hanging on the railing, on the wall's edge, viewing us, but for a change from the people in Flekkefjord and Kristiansand, they did not give us any good advice.

The public in Falmouth have been very hospitable and pleasant, and have taken a great interest in us. We have only the best memories to take with us from here. This afternoon we took a cruise around the harbor and among other sights we saw the old clipper ship "Cutty Sark." She has been bought from the Portugese by an Englishman and is laying here now, and I believe occasionally used as a training ship for boys. What memories, what tales, what romance cling to the name "Cutty Sark." It is pleasant to know that she is still on the water "going strong."

No day in the lifetime of "TradeWind" has she had so many visitors as today. Young and old, rich and poor, men and women. It seems to me that the whole population of this town must have been down here today and some of them more than once. Well, it's nice, but it gets on one's nerves to have a hundred eyes on one all the time. At sea it is only us—nature and the peaceful thoughts of a contented mind.

Friday 28 April 1933. We came afloat at 7 a.m. and proceeded to our old moorings. It was our intention to start on across the Biscay today, but it is raining and the wind has veered to S. No matter; each thing has its time and place. So also with the weather.

Today has been a quiet day. No excitement of any description. Different from yesterday when we had to cope with a half-hundred curious visitors at a time. A large percentage of yesterday's guests were girls. Alwine and Doreen and the rest of the lovely "things." In the afternoon the wind calmed down and veered to the usual S.W. It has been raining since morning.

Falmouth 28-4-33 H. M. H.

This is one of the two sea anchors on the TradeWind during its Atlantic crossing. Round and made of canvas, it was thrown overboard to operate like a parachute, slowing the boat during stormy weather such as the Hamrans encountered in the Bay of Biscay.

The Dreaded Bay of Biscay

"The odds are very much against our getting through this."

Saturday 29 April 1933. At 8 a.m. we cast loose from our moorings, filled our fresh-water barrels to the top from a floating crane, and accepted an invitation from a tugboat to "hang on" as they were going about 4 miles out into the bay.

People on the boats and ships in the harbor waved their hats and caps and arms at us, and shouted, wishing us "good luck." We passed out of the narrows with the old castle-like forts on both sides. Green fields and green trees—Merrie England. The English have been friendly to us and have taken a big interest in us and our boat. More in fact than the Norwegians. So it is with a touch of regret that we leave this pleasant Falmouth. The local paper here had pictures of us in today's issue.

So *au revoir* Falmouth. Good luck Old England. You deserve the very best of luck and prosperity. Stray clouds and a S.W. wind. Sunshine and hail and now and then a little rain squall. April showers. We are beating south to clear the Lizard.

Sunday 30 April 1933. Small breeze from S.S.W. Occasional squalls. Course from midnight W.S.W. Speed about 3 knots. Lizard light abeam at 5:15 a.m. Distant about 10 miles.

Wind changed to south about noon. Course S.W.

Sunshine, rain, and a breeze from the south. Cornwall (Lands End and Lizard Point) in northeast not visible because covered by clouds of which the lower are blue-gray and violet and the higher white and gray and red and in fantastic shapes. Good-bye England.

Monday 1 May 1933. Small breeze from S. Course S.W. Speed about 3 miles. Departure taken yesterday from Lizard light. 49.57.40. N. 5.12.6.W. at noon. Saw reflection of Bishop light at 4 a.m. About 70 miles S.W. of Lands End at noon today. Between 6 and 8 p.m. the wind freshened and turned easterly. At 11:30 we laid in a reef in the mainsail. Free sheets. Course S.W. Speed about 6 miles.

Tuesday 2 May 1933. We have had an unpleasant night. From midnight to morning the wind increased to storm. High sea and lots of whitecaps. For staysail and reefed mainsail running before the wind. Rain poured down in torrents. Thunder and lightning. Balls of light (stormlights) fastened themselves on the masttop and another on the peak of my cap. I must have looked weird like a spook to my partner as I stood at the wheel and this little nutshell of a boat was running like a mad thing in between breaking mountainous seas.

Around noon the wind veered southeast and later on S. and calmed down considerably. In the afternoon a fresh breeze. Course S.W. Sailed since yesterday noon 90 miles.

So this is the Bay of Biscay!

Wednesday 3 May 1933. Wind turned to S.W. and storm. We reefed down our sails but had to take them in at 5:30 a.m. as our vessel could not carry sails. Put out sea anchor at 5:30 a.m. and laid for it head to the wind till 12 noon. The weather then had moderated a little, and for staysail and reefed mainsail we kept her head to the wind doing about 3 knots on a course W.S.W. At 5 p.m. wind and sea, however, forced us to lay her once more for sea anchor. Windstorm from W.S.W.

Thursday 4 May 1933. Storm from S.S.W. High seas. For sea anchor. At 12 o'clock noon we reefed her down and for a couple small traces of canvas stood a course of S.S.E. Speed about 4 miles.

We spent a miserable night last night. We were tossed about terribly. It was hopeless to try to sleep as we were tossed clear out of the bunks. It was almost as bad to sit down.

The seas washed over us continually and we leaked a lot. Outside the wind sang in the rigging like a thousand mournful harps. In weather like this, one realizes what a little nutshell the "TradeWind" really is. We looked small and insignificant between mountainous seas. Hope the weather will calm down a little tonight.

Well, this is the Bay of Biscay! It is 11 o'clock p.m. after we have sailed 45 miles S.E. The odds are very much against our getting through this. Our chances are slim, but no matter. It's great to take chances when all things are against one. And we have lived—also in this voyage.

Friday 5 May 1933. From yesterday noon beating up to Cape Finisterre. At 6 o'clock a.m. laid her on starboard tack, having done 35 miles W.S.W. Sailed till 11 a.m. when a strong wind and mountainous seas compelled us to lay her for sea anchor once more. Sailed 25 miles S.S.E. to 11 a.m.

At 6 p.m. we double-reefed our mainsail and with staysail we again tried to see if she could make any headway. Rain in torrents—squalls. Course S.S.E. Speed 5 miles.

Saturday 6 May 1933. A never-ending succession of storm clouds comes hurtling out of the gloom from S.W.

Storm. High seas. Course S. Speed 5. At 9:50 this morning we sighted a lot of ships. We are probably outside Cape Finisterre or Cape Ortegal. In this onshore wind and sea, we dare not try to get near Sisargas Island or Cape Villano.

At 4 p.m. the wind died down suddenly. We seemed to be located in the center of a revolving storm as the wind blew with great force, changing twice round the compass during one hour.

In the evening it cleared and we got a fine breeze from W.N.W. And although a heavy sea was running, the weather was good— for the first day in a long while. Course S.W. Speed 8 miles. This Bay of Biscay!

Sunday 7 May 1933. A fine small breeze from W.N.W. Moonlight and clear. We sailed S.W. till 5 a.m. Speed 7 miles.

We were dead tired and all our clothes and blankets were wet. We could not keep our eyes open. So with only the staysail to keep her head before the wind, we "turned in" and slept till 12 noon.

At 12 noon we set sail for a course of S. Speed 6 1/2 miles and kept on that course till 8 p.m. when the breeze slackened off and our course was altered to E. During the night a light fog came on. Today is the finest day we have had on our voyage so far.

Monday 8 May 1933. Light fog. Small breeze from W.N.W. Hardly enough to stiffen the sail bunting. Course E. Our speed 2 1/2 and at times 3 miles.

Altered course to S.E. at noon and to S.S.W. at 1:30 p.m. as the wind is freshening and a haze makes visibility poor. We do not want to be caught on a "lee shore" if it can be prevented.

We are traveling along at 7 miles, 7:45 p.m. We are traveling ahead at a good speed, considering our size. This "Biscayan Wester" is an even wind and very pleasant to sail with, as it is so reliable.

Tomorrow, if it's clear weather, we will make our course more easterly so we can get bearing of land—"land hungry."

Tuesday 9 May 1933. Clear skies, a warm sun, and a small breeze from N.W. Course E. Speed 2 miles.

This morning an English destroyer (12) passed us close by, going south. They probably wondered what our business would be in these parts of the world.

Today our whole deck is littered with wet clothes—to dry. And what a mess the Bay of Biscay made of our effects. Clothes, charts, provisions—all are damaged more or less. No matter. It is nothing to be grumbling over. We had to be and were prepared for the worst.

Wednesday 10 May 1933. Warm. Calm sea. No wind. Occasional glimpses of fishing smacks. Seeing land would do me good. Moon went down in a clear atmosphere—so transparent, in fact, that the last rim was plainly in view till it disappeared below the horizon.

A glorious sunrise, "a picture in colors."

Seldom, if ever, have I seen such a heavy swell as today. It sounds like exaggeration, but it is between 400-500 yards from one top to another. The height I judge to be 25-30 feet. It reminds me of the rolling prairies. One is just hankering after taking a walk over these "sea prairies." They do not look like sea at all.

We saw a large shark today. He was swimming around slowly with the fin out of water. Saw also driftwood and parts of fishing corklines. And porpoises have been playing and frolicking around us all day. A sunny southern day. Gentle breeze from W.N.W. since noon. At 5:45 p.m. we sighted land. It was Les Balines between Bordeaux and Bayonne in Lat. 46°15' N. °34' W. Tide, current, and stormy weather have set us into the bay.

Thursday 11 May 1933. Course W. . Wind N.N.W. Speed 5 miles. 10 p.m. Cape Higuer S.E. Cape Machichaco S.W.

Friday 12 May 1933. In a dead calm. Close inshore on the west side of Cape Machichaco 43°27' N. L. 45° W.

It has been a fine day. I have corked (calked) the deck and dried the charts and other wet effects. Among the Spanish sardine fishing fleet. Have waved my arms in greeting so much today that I feel tired in them.

Rocks, cloisters, mountains, and tilled fields. This part of Spain reminds me of California. We are having easy days now. Hope we get past Bilbao tonight.

Saturday 13 May 1933. Warm and fine. Between Castro Urdiales and Cape Mayor. The sea alive with sardines. Hundreds of small fishing smacks. The sea here seems alive with all sorts of sea creatures. Perhaps it is the warm sun that tempts all life up to the surface. Sardines, jellyfish, crabs the size of a beetle (1/3 of an inch), porpoises, and seabirds, and fish only a half-inch long.

The land here is magnificent. Steep mountains and green tilled valleys, old castles, and cloisters (convents). The land of the old conquistadores and bold seamen. Sunny Spain fallen from her old position as the mistress of the world. How we humans are wonderful and yet almost stupid to madness.

At 10:45 p.m. we had Cape Mayor 43°30'N. 3°48'W. abeam. Distant 6 miles. Saw the lights of the city (Santander) but could not afford to port here. We must use this easterly breeze as well as we can.

Sunday 14 May 1933. The forenoon was dead calm. Not a gust of wind. Laying about 12 miles N.W. of Santander. Lots of whales and large ones. Must have seen 12-15 today.

In the afternoon a light easterly breeze. Course W. At 6 p.m. Cape Mayor E. Distant 18 miles. Cloudy. Calm. Warm.

H.M.H.

Monday 15 May 1933. Fresh gale from the east. Following the coast and making great speed—around 8 knots. Course varying west-W.N.W.

This morning at 3 a.m. Ribadesella abeam. At 4 p.m. Cape Penas 43°39'N. 5°51'W. abeam. Continually passing through clusters of sardine fishing smacks. Life is sweet in this eastern wind. We are forging ahead and the Spaniards are all watching us and waving to us.

Tuesday 16 May 1933. The eastern wind died out between 8-10 a.m. 12 noon a fresh N.W. rose. Beating northwestward to clear the headlands (forelands). 4 p.m. Estaca Point abeam.

Got some cigarettes from a Spaniard today. Taste wonderful after having smoked tea for 2-3 days. "When you are tempted to overindulge, reach for a white rose tea cigarette." By jove, as Luckner says, it is all in a lifetime. But tea is poor stuff for smoking.

Spain! After all, there is no country like Spain. Something proud, something tragic is in the air of Spain. Memories of gallantry, of exquisite beauty, of daring, of romance. And the country is peculiarly inspiring. High mountains, green sloping fields, regular lines of trees and groves in the orchards. Steep cliffs on the coast. And monasteries and castles in profusion. And let no one think that Spain is a lazy decadent country. I do not think so. Here is hustle and bustle and the Spaniard is a virile person, perhaps a little more practical and sensible than most of us. He can work, but he loves the sun and life, too.

Wednesday 17 May 1933. Northeasterly fresh wind. Course W.S.W. Passed Cape Prior at 7 a.m. 12 noon Sisargas Island S.W. distant about 12 miles.

Sunshine, warm. Some traffic N. and S. Only one cigarette left for the two of us. I have just had a longing look at it, but decided to leave it for tonight. It will not be so long now before

33

we get a tobacco supply either in Vigo Bay or Lisbon.

1:45 p.m. Sisargas Island abeam, distant 6 miles.

At 4:15 p.m. altered course to S.

5:00 p.m. Cape Villano (43°10'N. 9°13'W.} abeam.

6:15 p.m. Cape Torinana abeam.

9:00 p.m. Cape Finisterre (42°53'N. 9°16'W.) abeam, distant 6 miles.

Thursday 18 May 1933. During the night the wind calmed down some and turned to N. Course S. by W. Passed Cape Cornbedo and Salvora and Arosa Islands. 8 a.m. found us west of Chis Island. This island light 42°13'N. 8°55'W. about 12 miles distant.

Around noon the wind became fresh from N. Course S. by W. Speed 5 1/2 miles.

Outside Vigo Bay. I get a kick out of watching my partner fill his pipe out of our tea can. His unshaven face is long and sad—almost tragic when time comes to "light up." I forget my own longing for a smoke in the humor of the situation and cannot help laughing. It is easier to bear than I imagined anyway.

Friday 19 May 1933. A gray cloudy day with a small breeze from N. Course S. Speed till noon 3 1/2 miles. At 8:15 a.m. altered course to S. by E. as we are on the outside of regular lanes. Passed Cape Mondego at 5 p.m. Pinedo da Sandade light abeam at 9 on A.C.S. Saw reflex in the sky of Burling light at 11 p.m.

Saturday 20 May 1933. Fitful northerly wind. At 4 a.m. Lesser Burling light looming up out of darkness on port bow. At 7 a.m. Great Burling light abeam. Course S. Speed 4 miles.

My partner is always having a mixup with Spanish names. Castro Urdinales *Blir* (becomes) Castor Urinales. Cape Penas *er ogsa noc forvsagt* (is also changed). Also Cape Buste becomes Cape Busted. Cape Ortegal *Kap Ogsågal* (Cape Also Crazy).

Seriously there is rhythm and music in the Spanish language. Take for instance those adventurous, romantic-sounding California names. Names like Sacramento, Los Angeles,

San Francisco. There is poetry in such names.

From noon fresh N.W. breeze. Course S.S.W. Sailed from noon to 6 p.m. 32 miles. At 6:45 p.m. we had Cape Roca 38°47'N. 9°30'W. abeam.

A Danish ship the "Marie" of Esbjerg steered close by and wished us *god reise* (good trip). Another ship, the "Nordlinge," waved and shouted greetings to us as they steamed past us N.

Steered into the harbor of Lisbon and tied up at 11:30 p.m. at the Shell Oil dock (wharf). Night clear and starry. Fresh breeze from N. The second *étappe* (leg) on the voyage done.

Lisbon 20 May 1933.

Sunday 21 May 1933. Sunshine and warm. After a cup of coffee, having had a peaceful night's sleep in port, we shifted to a basin further up in the harbor and there reported ourselves to the customs.

They telephoned to the Port health authorities and we had to sail out to the quarantine station again. At last everything was settled and in the afternoon we had a visit aboard of a couple of functionaries from D. A. Knudsen & Co. shipping agents. The customs assistant had telephoned them and they knew of our arrival.

Monday 22 May 1933. In port writing and sending letters. Wrote 11-12 pages for newspaper publication and sent it through Lars Hansen. A lot of curious visitors on the quay all day. Sunshine, clear, a lovely day.

H.M.H.

Tuesday 23 May 1933. In port of Lisbon. Cleaning water-casks and repairing rigging, and doing some alterations. 3 o'clock to Knudsen for purchase of provisions. A warm day. Finished writing here.   Lisbon 23-5-1933

Wednesday 24 May 1933. Have all provisions aboard. Weather fine. No mail from home. Shall fill fresh water now. Ready for departure.

Have been at Consulate. The consul is a real fine fellow and has smoothed over many of our difficulties here in Lisbon.

Lisbon is a peculiar town in an architectural way. On a square (plaza) fronted on the fourth side by the sea lies the old ministerial departments. Interior, marine, justice, supreme court (tribunal), finance, and post office. Wherever one goes there are always guards and soldiers, and all are armed with either rifle or revolver, and long bayonet. There are many old and fine buildings in this town and there are some remarkable statues and monuments. One of the most interesting, in a way, is the "helmsman."

Lisbon is an expensive town to buy things in—to live in. Some of our grumblers of high prices at home would drop dead if they knew the prices of commodities and foodstuffs in particular. Flour 0.62 øre package. Margarine (1st class) kroner 2.40 kilo. Olive oil 1.40 per liter. Sugar kroner 1.00 per kilo. and so on *ad infinitum.*

There are a lot of street-girls (prostitutes). In some quarters it is impossible to go 10 yards without being accosted by one of these, our fallen sisters. What a mess we humans make of this beautiful green world.

Lisbon 24/5/1933   Harald Hamran.

Deck Line

The Beautiful Canary Islands

Thursday 25 May 1933. At ten o'clock this morning, with a small breeze from N., we sailed out of the inner harbor of Lisbon. We passed the two Norwegian ships in port—the "Segovia" of Oslo and the "Estrella" of Bergen. The first-named one greeted us with her flag on. The other one had the whole crew gathered on the poop and they were wishing us "good luck" and "good voyage." The tide turned at 11:45 and we anchored up inside of Fort Julian, outer harbor, cooked our dinner, had a swim, and watched some bathers making fools of themselves on the beach. It's glorious to live. This is an ideal life, almost.

Lifted anchor at 4 p.m. 4:15 passed outer narrows. Wind fresh N. Course S.S.W. Speed 5 1/2 - 6 miles. Good-bye Lisbon. You weren't so bad after all. Especially have we only good memories of the Norwegian Consul. He was a gentleman and a sportsman.

At 8:15 p.m. Cape Espichel 30°25' N. 9°13' W. abeam. New moon is in view.

Friday 26 May 1933. Fresh wind from N. till 12 noon, course S. Speed 6 1/2 miles. At 12 noon departure taken from Cape St. Vincent 37°1' N. 9° 0' W. Course S.W. Distant 20 miles N.E.

An innumerable lot of porpoises play around and make the sea all aspray. Warm. Clear. Sailed till noon 97 miles S. by W.

Saturday 27 May 1933. Steady breeze from N.N.E. Course S.W. by W. Speed 4 to 5 miles. Sailed to noon 102 miles. Small good-weather wisps of fantastically formed clouds. Lots of drift matter—boxes, pieces of painted wood (white), and tins. All is well; moving along nicely. No ships in view so far. Painted the cabin deck this afternoon.

Sunday 28 May 1933. Steady N.N.E. Clear. Sunshine. Course S.W. by W. Sailed to noon 106 miles. A blue heaven and a blue sea. The only life is the storm petrel that skips from one wavetop to another. My partner had another culinary accident today. He got the flapjack-makings all over his clothes and broke some dishes. It is pretty tough to be cook aboard the "TradeWind."

Monday 29 May 1933. Fresh N.E. wind. Same sea. Sailed to noon 136 miles. Course S.W. by W.

There are quite a lot of some transparent rainbow-like "blaere" fish (jellyfish) floating around. They are about 4-6 inches long and tagged like the comb of a rooster. Some 3 inches is out of water. They burn badly when touched.

We bought 200 cigars in Lisbon and they are—terrible. Almost as bad as tea to smoke. When Hans lights up it's time to get on the wind side of him.

Wish I had some good old "Edgeworth." Well, the Portugese cigars will have to do for awhile.

Tuesday 30 May 1933. Wind fresh N.E. Course S.W. by 1/2 W. Sailed to noon 115 miles. Saw quite a few ships. A royal Mail-Passenger ship passed us homeward bound last night. Getting near the Canary Islands.

At 7:30 p.m. Fredrik Olsen Co.'s "San Carlos" passed us only half a cable length away. Everybody was on deck and waved to us and wished us a "good voyage." Sportsmanship and seamanship have always been to the fore in that company. Thank you! May you have all kinds of luck.

Wednesday 31 May 1933. Wind light N.E. Course S.W. Sailed to noon 98 miles. Delicate whitish clouds and a blue-blue sky. The sea dark blue. Saw the first swarm (school) of flying fish today. Distance sailed from Lisbon to noon today 649 miles, exclusive of current. (Guinea current setting S. 12 m.p.d.)

At 4:30 p.m. we sighted a mountainous island on our starboard bow (W). It is too early yet to say which of the Canary Islands it is. I only hope it is Teneriffe. It should be by our reckoning.

It was Anaga Point, Teneriffe Island. We laid in a calm all night, but sailed past Santa Cruz (S).

Thursday 1 June 1933. Sailing west with a weak breeze on the southern coast of Teneriffe Island. The island presents a wild and moonlike appearance on this southern side. I counted from one view 44 volcanic craters and hillocks. The highest reach the great height of 12,180 feet o.t.s.

It is my 38th birthday today. A birthday in the midst of a great adventure. Twenty-one years ago I was here in an English ship. I could not then dream that I would reappear like this.

At 3 o'clock in the afternoon, sailing S.W. by the coast, we found a small town, under the mighty Mount Teneriffe, that looked inviting. We steered in and some of the townspeople came out with a heavy anchor for us as this is no port and the holding bottom is poor. We accepted the anchor and the friendship and good will of the people. The little town's name is Los Christianos. There is a person, the manager of a factory, who speaks very good English and it is well, as our Spanish is very poor and leaves much to be desired.

Friday 2 June 1933. In port writing to Lars Hansen and home. A wonderful day, sunshine and breeze and a calm sea.

They tell us in town that there is a Norwegian lady living in a village high up under Mount Teneriffe. Wish I could see her and talk to her.

Caught an octopus today, in the harbor by the boat. The natives got it as they eat them. These sea creatures are considered a great delicacy by the natives. It wasn't so small, either, as it measured 4 feet between the sucking arms.

Saturday 3 June 1933. In Los Christianos for anchor. Finished writing. A lovely day with sunshine and a cool breeze. Bought provisions for the trip and it was quite a job to make the Spanish shopkeeper know our wants.

Sunday 4 June 1933. We have had a day full of adventure. At 8 a.m. there arrived boat after boat loaded with natives. They took charge of our whole boat. Set out numberless anchors and cables and swarmed all over the deck and rigging. Those who could get no space to stand on deck were in their boats alongside.

Then the fun began. They hauled our "TradeWind" on the sandy beach and scrubbed the bottom and sides and painted her bottom in no time. Then they had ordered dinner for us, in advance, at the only restaurant in the little village, and paid for it as our hosts. It was a good dinner—soup, omelettes, chicken, potatoes, salad, fish, sweets, coffee, cigars, and imported Dutch beer. The only real civilized meal since we started the voyage two months ago.

Childish, but wonderful, honest, and sympathetic people. Nowhere else have I met people like those here in this little town on Teneriffe Island. So today has been like a holiday—a feast day. Even if the worst should happen a day like this is worth many years of trouble and difficulties.

I should especially mention three brothers Milo. They have been extraordinarily good, friendly, and helpful. There are only the best of memories of Teneriffe. In the afternoon they set our vessel out and there must have been at least 200 people there. Those that could not get near enough to push on our boat stood alongside and gave orders, young and old of both sexes.

They brought aboard bananas, tomatoes, cigars, and wine, and were extraordinarily friendly. They even got hold of our mail and posted it and paid the postage (2.50).

At dinner in the hotel we looked terrible in our homemade canvas trousers and brown faces and scrubby long whiskers, and yet sitting at the same table as two well-dressed Spanish gentlemen, we seemed to have all the interest and attention. It's a queer world and a wonderful green world we live in if we will only see it.

Monday 5 June 1933. Ready to start. A fine day. Finishing the last letters. Hans is painting. This Teneriffe is a paradise to live in, but we have to tear ourselves loose and be on our way.

The people of these islands are as yet unspoiled. There are very few factories and the islands are agricultural. Can only be compared to some of the South Sea islands. Sun, breeze, fruit, wine, vegetables, fowl, and fish, and a friendly, appealing population.

The Canary Islands!

West of Morocco on the coast of Africa in about Latitude 27° N. Longitude 12-17° are these islands with their wonderful climate. The main islands from east to west are Lanzarote, Fuerteventura, Grand Canary, Teneriffe, Gomera, Ferro (Hierro), and farther west, Palma, and some very small rocks and desert islands. They belong to Spain and the young men of the isles do military service in Spain in the year they reach 21 years.

The islands are rocky and of a volcanic structure, but nevertheless very fertile. The mountains of the island are awe-inspiring. The loftiest peak is found on the Island of Teneriffe and reaches an altitude of 12,180 feet, an enormous height considering that the size of the island is less than 200 square miles. I could count from a single place of observation no fewer than 44 volcanic mounds and mountains on the south side of Teneriffe Island.

The climate is wonderful and healthy. Many people with lung disease have regained health by living in the pure Canarian air. There are three towns of any size, Las Palmas on Grand Canary, Santa Cruz de Teneriffe, and another Santa Cruz on Palma Island (Santa Cruz de Palmas).

Fruit, wine, vegetables, and tobacco are produced in large quantities. The people are unbelievably friendly and hospitable. In many ways these islands and their people remind me of some of the more favored of the South Sea Islands.

The people are cleanly and honest. Watching them handle their small and neat fishing boats or seeing the younger generation swimming or playing in the water or on the beach is a treat.

Sunburned, dark-eyed, appealingly friendly Canaries! Of you we will have only the best of memories. Your lofty mountains, your villages high up on the mountainsides, your warm breezy nights.

So the people and their land are one of the few unspoiled in these days when the world, its people, and its systems seem to be all wrong.

This afternoon several boats of people set out from shore and rowed out to us. They had with them presents in the form of cigars, bread, fish, and postcards or photographs.

Finished a long letter to Lars Hansen and posted it today.

Hope something can be made from it in a monetary way, as we will need it badly on our arrival in New York.

Los Christianos 5 June 1933 HMH

Tuesday 6 June 1933. The usual lovely weather. About 6 a.m. the natives are awake and bustle around with their small fishing boats. Others take it more quietly and sit on the ground in gatherings of from 5-6 or 15-20, smoking and talking. At 7 a.m. some start to work and at 8 others do so, and they work like they are playing. In the afternoon they will lie down in the shade or in their cool rooms and enjoy their siesta. The shops cannot be noticed from the street—not even the largest ones. There are no goods or wares on display in the windows.

The children, of which there are a great number, are on the beach almost the whole day, playing or in the sea swimming. Boys and girls are almost invariably apart. When the girls go for a swim, which they do about once a day, they are always on a different part of the beach. Bathing suits are not common, but can be seen now and then. The children swim remarkably fast and well.

This is the dry season in these islands and where there is no water the earth is a lava-brown-red color. But one does not notice these things much in town because the girls here are very nice looking and well-built. Maybe the women get their figures from carrying weights on the head. All burdens, whether fish baskets, water, or baskets of fruit, are always borne on the head. I have seen small tots only 3 or 4 years old carry baskets of fish or fruit on their heads.

All day the natives have been asking us what time we are leaving. When told that we are leaving in the afternoon they rowed ashore and started getting busy. Boat after boat (no fewer than 15 of them) put off from shore with from two to four persons in each, and brought us as gifts several dozen eggs, some 30 kilos of potatoes, tomatoes, several bottles of wine, a large basket of bread, 3 or 4 dozen real good cigars, matches, fish, chocolates, and postcards and photos.

Willing hands hoisted sails and anchors for us, and we were followed out from the coast by a host of small sailboats. Six of them followed us far out to sea. Sunny Canaries—hospitable, friendly people. Maybe of all places and all the people we have met, we'll remember you the longest. One could almost forgive any fault in such a people.

And the sea is dark blue and the sky is of a much lighter hue with red and white clouds here and there. Up on the hillsides are many, many small villages and green gardens and plantations, while crowning all on this beautiful green island is Mount Teneriffe 12,180 feet o.t.s.

How wonderful to have health, to be free, to court danger and adventure and romance in this beautiful green sunny world. So good-bye Teneriffe. Good-bye Canary islands. Only the best of memories of you remain with us. And if the good will and good wishes and tender thoughts of a visitor count for anything with you, you have it all.

Our friends from shore, who followed us out from the coast, had fireworks with them and kept up a regular fusillade the whole time. At parting we said good-bye both personally, and later with our flag when they were returning home.

6 p.m. in a calm halfway between Teneriffe and Gomera Island. Course W.

A wonderful sunset with the islands Teneriffe, Palma, Gomera and Ferro (Hierro) in sight, the first-named green, the others further away, lofty, and blue skies, red and gold, rosy and yellow, white and violet. One could almost imagine oneself transplanted to another strange, colorful, more congenial world.

The Canaries! As some think, the last remnant of the lost continent of Atlantis.

Liquid compass is round and slightly below deck level.

Crossing the Atlantic

"We'll certainly beat Columbus hands down."

Wednesday 7 June 1933. Variable breeze in here between the islands. Course W. by S. Nearly full moon now, so we had very bright moonlight last night. At noon, halfway between Gomera and Ferro (Hierro), Teneriffe's mountains are visible above the layers of clouds. Appear similar to Mount Rainier in the state of Washington, U.S.A. Nearly full moon now so had very bright moonlight last night. At noon Mount Teneriffe N.N.E., Ferro W., Gomera N.W. Had a smoke of our Los Christianos friends' cigars today. They are good. At 8:15 p.m. the highest peak on Teneriffe was still dimly visible, although we were a great distance away. At 10:30 p.m. had sailed down Ferro Island. Moonlight. Clear with stray clouds over the land. Starry. Warm. Course W.S.W. Sailed to noon, 45 miles.

Thursday 8 June 1933. Uneven N.E. Course W.S.W. Flying fish seen, but not in great numbers. A fish about 18 inches long, gray-blue in color with black rings around the body, is following the boat. Sailed to noon 65 miles.

Friday 9 June 1933. We are getting a more even breeze now. Are probably getting into the regular N.E. "trades." My partner is in poor condition because of a weak stomach. Am doctoring the best I know how, but it does not help very much.

Days are warm, with sun and light-hued stray clouds. Are moving around and living naked except around noon when the sun is too hot and the body needs covering. Lovely days and nights. Full moon (on the 8th) and starry nights. "God, it's a glorious life to live."

Course W.S.W. Sailed to noon 63 miles. A Dutch ship passed us at a distance of a half-mile, going S.W. 5 o'clock. Yellow smokestack, blue band with a white star.

Saturday 10 June 1933. We are both of us a little sickly. Have probably overdone the sun-bathing. Several ships have gone by, all heading S.W. (S.S.W.). Rigged foresails crosswise. Wind N.E. Course W.S.W. Sailed to noon 83 miles. Heavy cross-swell S. and N.N.E. Moon nearly full (on wane), rises at midnight.   Harald Magnus Hamran

Sunday 11 June 1933. We are within the regular limits of the northeast trade (tradewinds). The wind is fresh and even N.E. Flying fish flew into our sails and fell on our deck last night, so in addition to our "flapjacks" and eggs this morning, we had fried fish. They are delicious. Reminds one of the taste of tender young mackerel. Fresh N.E. Course W.S.W. Sailed to noon 92 miles. W.S.W. Sunday noon 343 miles corrected offhand for error. S.W.

Monday 12 June 1933. Usual weather. This morning a school of a peculiar fish (not flying fish) came out of the sea and onto our deck. About a dozen remained on deck. My partner was at the helm and he certainly became interested in these fish. His breakfast was cold when his fish study was over.
Wind fresh N.E. Course W.S.W. Sailed to noon 118 miles.

Tuesday 13 June 1933. Even N.E. Many flying fish. Strong S.W. current. Course W.S.W. Sailed to noon 102 miles. At 6 o'clock I altered the course to W. as I considered we were far enough south to get a regular even N.E. over to the West Indies.
W.S.W. Corrected for error S.W. 563 miles (sailed) + 57 miles (current) = 620 miles.   13-6-33 - Noon. S.W.

Wednesday 14 June 1933. Course W. Wind fresh N.E. Sailed to noon 122 miles. There are many incidents in connection with this trip I can never forget. Evenings when after a beautiful sunset and the wind is still fresh, little "TradeWind" seems to do her best in regard to speed. The wind is caressing, mild and in bright moonlight (now waning) the sea is silvery and our snow-white sails furnish a wonderful contrast. To steer our "TradeWind" is like handling a thing alive. Running before the wind with it on the starboard quarter, she sets the forepart down and lifts the stern when going fast or riding seas.

In case of riding seas, it is necessary to have her under good control. But it is not particularly difficult as she answers the helm well.

"Oh I'm the wind that sailors love. I'm strongest at noon,
Yet under the moon, I'm filling a bunting of sail."
—*The Sea Wolf,* by Jack London.

The sea in this part of the world is not like at home up in "the roaring forties." Yet I love it, and life at sea, and especially now, is sweet. Wonderful, beautiful world. A day of pleasure is worth a year of sorrow.

One moment of the well of life to taste,
The next into annihilations waste.

But it's worth it, and I am satisfied and thankful.

Thursday 15 June 1933. Wind fresher than usual. N.E. Course W. Sailed to noon 131 miles.

Nothing much doing nowadays except eating (cooking), steering, and taking sunbaths. In fact I am nearly all day without any clothes on. It is more comfortable and one feels very light and free in body and mind when after the first sunburn one gets used to the sun. The only life visible is flying-fish of which there are a lot. Often they fly against the sails and fall on our deck.

We are dividing the day into five watches. 12 noon to 6, 6-12 or two 6-hour watches; from midnight to 4 a.m., 4 to 8, and 8 to 12 noon. Breakfast is made by watch below 8-12, lunch by watch below 12-6, dinner the same watch below around 5-5:30.

We have a little yard rigged out abeam from the mastchair and on the outer end of this we sail our jib. Have made a loose stay (separate from rigging) for the staysail and use that sail crosswise on our "forecastlehead." So all our canvas is drawing.

Wind and sun! We will certainly be sunburned and bewhiskered by the time we reach New York. I am of a mind that we will not be very presentable. In all probability we will look like a couple of old-time pirates who have been on a long voyage without finding any prey. Never mind, though! We are as good as pirates any time.   H. M. Hamran

Friday 16 June 1933. Fresh N.E. Course W. Sailed to noon 129 miles.

We are in the regular path of the Northeast "Trade." The wind is fresh day and night. From 8 o'clock or thereabouts in the morning the breeze freshens up and keeps even till around 6-8 in the evening around sundown, when it weakens a little. A bit of sea but nothing to mention. Like a channel sea when an ordinary breeze is blowing. The current here is strong and is easily seen and seems to bear W.S.W. (True).

We have no log, no chronometer, no sextant. So I am depending only on dead reckoning. I judged distance and current perfectly from San Julian (Lisbon) to Anaga Rocks (Teneriffe).

Our compass is not corrected and adjusted. I do that myself by taking bearings of the Pole star. The variation on our charts is not to be depended on, as they are old (one from 1911, the other from 1925). But I have no doubt about the outcome, as I have perfect confidence in my ability to judge these things. Guess I have been so long a seaman that I know the trade well. Sail and a little of steam.

Should be in Lat. 18 N. Long. 33 W. or thereabouts now. Nights dark and starry with stray white clouds.

In the Atlantic 16-6-33 18° N. 33° W. —Harald M. Hamran

Saturday 17 June 1933. Course W. Wind varying fresh N.E. to E.N.E. Sailed to noon 125 miles.

Nothing to do except getting bewhiskered and suntanned. Just to strip and move around without clothes to hamper one's movements. There are no passengers to consider—just God, nature, and our small, insignificant selves. And life is sweet living it this way. One almost feels oneself back in the days of the Spanish traffic to the "Spanish Main." We have no radio to bother us, either. My partner had a mandolin (and a good one, too) but it opened up in the seams and the strings rusted away so it was offered to father Neptune in the Bay of Biscay. That gentleman probably got busy with mandolin-playing as we had fine weather almost continually after that. Well, we are doing well, forging ahead splendidly considering the size of vessel and sailpower. We may not be in competition with the "Bremen" or the "Europa" for the blue ribbon of the Atlantic, but we'll certainly beat Columbus hands down.

At 12 o'clock midnight altered the course to W. by N.

Sunday 18 June 1933. Course W. by N. Wind more easterly than usual, fresh E.N.E. Sailed to noon 116 miles.

A sea bird the size of a seagull but with a very long narrow tail has been following us and hovering around all day. Our true followers, the aforementioned blue-gray fish with black rings around the body, are always with us. They are not so large as the first we noticed. These are about 15 inches long, but must have a large energy following us day after day across the Atlantic. What they live on is a mystery. Lots of flying fish but of small size. Too small to be of use as food.

They fly over our boat and several times have flown and hit the one of us who happens at the moment to be at the helm. And it hurts, even if they are small, especially when admiring the silvery moon and thinking of a dream girl ashore, to be rudely awakened by a flying fish in the eye. Last night was dark and cloudy and the day has been breezy and warm. We are getting very dark-hued from the sun.

Monday 19 June 1933. Wind E.N.E. Rather weak. Course W. by N. Sailed to noon 98 miles.

We should be halfway and more across the Atlantic now. Hope that the wind keeps fresh and blows us across in another 8-10 days.

We are living all right and do our best cooking. The boat is comparatively steady as we usually have the wind in a little on our starboard quarter and consequently sail for free sheets.

Potatoes, onions, vegetables, fresh and dried, different kinds of canned meats, flour, biscuits, sugar, butter, olive oil, and coffee. Our eggs were used up yesterday. Well, never mind! We have yet plenty of tobacco, cigars, cigarettes, and food, and our drinking water keeps cool, sweet, and fresh. And we have a bottle or two of wine left, so everything is O.K. How many tied-up slaves, rich and poor, would not envy us our life now?

A wonderful sunset in bright and many colors. Red, purple, violet, yellow, and white, and a blue of a tint only seen in sunsets in southern climes. Then it is dark, and in the south, outstanding for form and brightness among thousands of stars, is the Southern Cross, lower than the Polaris in the North, yet clear and bright. And one steers and dreams and remembers and recollects many things. Some that have departed for the "kingdom of stillness" from which there is no comeback. "The loveliest and the best." And the thoughts may dwell with a might-have-been. Yet it is great and wonderful to live, to think and work and dream, to hope that life will be full in this glorious sunny green.

Tuesday 20 June 1933. Wind weak E.N.E. Course from 4 a.m. W.N.W. Sailed to noon 70 miles.

If the sunset was glorious last night, the sunrise this morning was no less so. We have not altered the time since we left the Canary Islands so we are a little out from the usual way in comparing our clock to daylight and sun. But it does not matter as we have no navigation to consider. No sextant or chronometer or tables. For that matter, an old alarm clock would serve us just as well.

In the Atlantic in about Lat. 16° N. Long. 41° W.   H.M.H.

Wednesday 21 June 1933. Wind E.N.E. Course W.N.W. Sailed to noon 76 miles.

It may be a result of the isolation from other fellow beings that one in a carefree way philosophizes over life's problems, especially on nights when thousands of stars twinkle and the gentle warm rift of the Northeast tradewind fills the sail bunting and caresses one's face. Or other nights when a silvery moon is shining and on a dark-blue sea our little sailboat, with her snow-white sails, looks like a dream.

There is no loneliness aboard. We have lots to read, and do a little writing, and more than half of the time is occupied with those things, and in addition comes cooking, steering, and keeping a rude sort of dead-reckoning (navigation).

The breeze is not as fresh now as near the Canaries and Cape Verde Islands.

Thursday 22 June 1933. Wind E. Course from noon W. Sailed to noon 93 miles. We see stray white clouds that for a moment hide the sun in the daytime, and stray clouds of a darker hue at night that occasionally carry with them a few drops of rain as they pass by. But a blue sky in daytime and clear spaces with bright stars at nighttime is always to be seen in some direction. Nights are nice and cool but days are rather warm. Wonderful sunrises and sunsets almost every day. Wind a little fresher today than usual.

22-6-33. (1835 miles) W.S.W.

Friday 23 June 1933. Wind E. Course W. Sailed to noon 109 miles. A large quantity of seaweed. An oil tanker eastbound passed us at 1:30 a.m. The first ship observed for over half a month. We sailed without lights and passed the ship close by and probably were not observed aboard her.

A few birds are seen occasionally, but the sea is alive with flying fish. Some of them are so tiny, only an inch long, that they appear like silvery flecks of spray when they take to the air. They fly only 4 to 5 yards and less at a time. The large ones 4 to 10 inches long, can stay in the air for a full 3/4ths of a minute and can fly up to 400 yards at a time.

Strong current setting west by north. Air fresh and giving an ideal sailing breeze.

Saturday 24 June 1933. Wind E. Course W. Sailed to noon 115 miles. Today has been the warmest day since we started the voyage. If it continues, then we may have to set up awnings for our protection against the heat. We have both canvas bags and blankets to choose from, so it's not difficult to rig up some sort of awning.

Tonight is midsummer-eve. To celebrate, we had our last wine and some fruit. Many fond memories are connected with this day. Memories from Tunneshaugen and Halsen, from Tromsø, its heather and silver birches, from the days when we were young and all of us happy and "home." When we used to make "fires" on the 24th of June each year and the enormous columns of smoke rose mountain-high. And the air was murky for days after, if it was fine weather.

Oh, ah that spring should vanish with the rose,
That youth's sweet-scented manuscript should close.

Midsummer night! A fond greeting to all living and with sad memories of the loved ones who have passed away.

And I remember the "old days" when there were sailing ships on the ocean and *seters* (chalets) on every farm. The "old days" when there were large virgin forests in the old homeland and there were *huldre* and *drang* and *troll*.

The "old days" when people ate pure bread, meat, fish, and butter. Not living off teeth-destroying chewed canned stuff. There was something homey, cozy, romantic, and appealing about those days. Perhaps with our overbragged civilization we are only fools, a generation that more than any other has been living artificially—empty. No matter. Tonight all my thoughts are with *you* and *you* and back in my own youthful years.

In the Atlantic Ocean. Approx. Lat. 16° N. Long. 51° W.

24-6-1933. Harald Hamran

Sunday 25 June 1933. Wind E. Course W. Sailed to noon 109 miles.

At 12 noon we laid over on the starboard tack as the wind veered a little and because she sails better on the starboard tack. Both by the wind and before the wind she makes more headway on starboard tack.

The seaweed we saw so much of some days ago has now disappeared completely. Wind fresh and not much animal life with the exception of flying fish, of which there are a lot.

Monday 26 June 1933. Wind E. Course W. by N. Sailed to noon 90 miles.

Variation has been now for a couple of days 15° W. As marked on the charts formerly farther east it was 19° W.

Should soon be in a region where the variation is only 10° W. and if noticed, is a moment in calculating longitude. By our dead reckoning we should be in approximate latitude 16°N. longitude 54°W.

We are not to be recognized from before—suntanned to the

color of bronze and with beards that have been allowed to grow wild since we left Falmouth, England. If our friends and family could see us now, they would certainly not recognize us. The days pass by in sun and wind, with eating and sleeping and reading and now and then cracking jokes at our own expense in regard to sunburn, whiskers, and cooking abilities. We have some good books aboard: *Shakespeare's Complete Works*, Fitzgerald's *Omar Khayam*, some of Jack London's books, Goethe's *Faust*, some of Lars Hansen's books, Ibsen's *Brand* and *Peer Gynt*, Heinrich Heine, and Norwegian verse and other reading not so classical. This trip has been to me the most interesting event in my life. And in former years I have, I guess, had my full share of adventure and pleasure, joy and adversity. As the Yankees say: "It is great to be alive and kicking."

(26/6 W.S.W. 2258 + sur)

Tuesday 27 June 1933. Wind E. by N. Course to noon W. From noon N.W. by W. Sailed to noon 116 miles.

Wind fresh and very strong current setting approximately W. by N. Choppy sea a result of the heavy current. Altered the course at noon as considered far enough south and counting on being not far off Puerto Rico or the Virgin Islands. Visibility is not very good—from 10-15 miles. Nights starry and stray whitish clouds and cloud dots passing with the "eastern" overhead. New moon making visibility good at night.

Wednesday 28 June 1933. Wind E. (fresh). Course W.N.W. Sailed to noon 112 miles. A strong current is setting W.N.W. (True). Very choppy sea. Heavy swell of the current.

One needs be a juggler to make a meal these last two days. Yes, one must be a juggler to make a meal nowadays. No matter. Somehow, we manage anyway, despite burns, blisters, and some well-chosen words.

Sailor's life is a dog's life? I don't think so. It's a great, proud life, even if cooking, wind, weather, and bad-tasting "Mulligan" all are contrary.

Looking for land.

Thursday 29 June 1933. Wind E.N.E. Course from 12 midnight W. Sailed to noon 92 miles.

A beautiful sunset was seen last night. Many colors and fantastically shaped clouds, and as a "finale" the whole sky east to west, north to south was rosy-red and orange. Today has been squally. At intervals, rain has poured down in torrents. By observation of the Polaris we are having a variation of 10° W. at present. Our water is keeping good—sweet, fresh, and cool. Nights are beautiful and peaceful, with moonlight till past midnight. Have plenty of food, water, and tobacco, plenty to read, and much to plan and dream about. So everything is O.K.

Friday 30 June 1933. Wind varying N.E. to S.E. Course W. by N. Sailed to noon 75 miles.

Squally with rain pouring down in large quantities in between. A heavy swell, probably the result of the current veering W.N.W. on reaching the coast of South America.

Observed many seabirds today. Lots of seaweed and flying fish. The last-named of small size, mostly. Had forgotten to wind up the watch so it stopped on us this morning. We had set it—about the time. As of today at noon, we have covered a distance of about 2,653 miles since leaving the Canary Isles.

H. M. Hamran

Saturday 1 July 1933. Land! West Indies.

Wind E. (squally during the night). Course W. Sailed to noon 107 miles.

The moon disappeared at around 1 a.m. but it was fairly light. With a little trouble, the compass could be seen without light. Throughout the night the one on watch kept a good lookout for land and breakers. The wind was fresh and a very heavy swell was running W.N.W., a result of current (probably).

At 6 o'clock in the morning we sighted land forward a little on our port bow. A green, low island with a higher, more mountainous one further south. We steered close to the shore and asked a couple of Negro fishermen in a small boat if it was the Virgin Islands. They affirmed this and told us it was Anguilla, one of the British group in this area. We steered into a cozy little bay where large palm trees and coconut trees rose above the small huts, and tied up to a little pier for an hour talking to a couple of white residents. At first they would not believe that we came all the way from Kristiansand in Norway. "No fear." But at last, having looked us over, our beards, and our windblown appearance, they got used to the idea.

What a feast to see green land again after the blue-gray rolling Atlantic. To see trees and hear other people talk and hear news of the world.

So we have done the "Pond" in less than 25 days. To be exact 24 days, 20 hours. Not so bad considering our size. We sailed around 3,115 miles, taking into reckoning the long southerly course (circle). Not great circle but opposite to that. Actually we sailed route distance from Teneriffe Canary Isles to Anguilla Virgin Isles 2,760 miles.

Left Anguilla at 10 a.m. for St. Thomas or Puerto Rico. Course West.   Anguilla, July 1, 1933. H. M. Hamran

Sunday 2 July 1933. We sailed for a fresh easterly breeze on a course of W. till at 6 a.m. we sighted St. Croix on our port bow. From 6:30 a.m. we laid a course of N. for Charlotte Amalie on St. Thomas and steered into the harbor there at 11:10 a.m.

Had the port health (quarantine) and customs aboard. They sent us a bill for $5 but they have not much chance of getting it. Had an invitation from a Danish resident to dinner tomorrow. Don't know if we'll go—whiskers, rags, and all.

Charlotte Amalie, St. Thomas. July 2, 1933.

Monday 3 July 1933. Had a peaceful night's rest in port with the scent of grass and shore in the nostrils.

Writing to Lars Hansen and home. Have rigged up the staysail as an awning, so feel comfortable in the offshore breeze.

Arriving by launch, the quarantine officers came aboard at 1 p.m. and started fumigating. My partner ashore to do the port business with consul, quarantine, customs, and the rest.

The harbormaster and the consul came to visit. The last named invited us to lunch at 12 noon tomorrow.

Finished fumigating at 5 p.m. At 6 p.m. had dinner with a

Danish resident who is employed here by the East Asiatic Co. Cocktails, Carlsberg beer, and a good dinner.

Must leave the rest of the writing till tomorrow. So for a good night's rest. *En natt i "havn"* (one night in the port).

Tuesday 4 July 1933. The American day of Independence and the town is decorated with flags.

Writing to L. Hansen. Had dinner-lunch at the Norwegian Consul at 2 p.m. A Danish resident, a Danish lady, the consul and his wife, a very pleasant Danish woman. Cocktails, good beer, and tasty appetizing food. What a difference to the result of our own efforts in the difficult art of good cooking. Never mind! It's bad but we are not poisoned of it, and after a month of living on our own food it tastes all the better having a real meal once in a blue moon.

And peaceful nights—sleeping on deck, Hans on the afterdeck and I on the forecastlehead (cabin roof), a breeze from the east, offshore, and a silver moon overhead in a setting of white clouds. How sweet is life.

Charlotte Amalie, St. Thomas, Virgin Islands. 4-7-33.

H. M. Hamran

The Deck Hatch

Sailing North to New York City

Wednesday 5 July 1933. Depart St. Thomas, Virgin Islands. At 9 o'clock went ashore and cleared the papers for our departure. Customs, Harbor Office, U. S. Public Health (fumigating) and received a favorable weather report from the U. S. Naval Radio Station to the effect that weather was fairly stable for the next 24 hours.

We decided to leave for New York. At one o'clock, we shifted to East-Asiatic Co.'s quay and took aboard a supply of fresh water, and paraffin for cooking purposes. Left at 2 p.m. by the shallow west passage. An English ship, the "Llannelly," steered close by to have a good look at us before it steamed N.E. At 3:15 abeam W. end St. Thomas Island. Course W.N.W. Wind weak E.N.E.

Thursday 6 July 1933. Fresh easterly wind. At 1 o'clock in the morning had abeam Vacia Talegas on the N.E. corner of Puerto Rico Island. Course W. N. W. At 5 a.m. we altered the course to W. by S. and steered for the city of San Juan de Puerto Rico to see if any storm signals were hoisted on the signal-mast at Morro Point. Passed Morro Point at 8:30 a.m. No storm warning signals. Altered course to N.W. At 12 noon Point Puerto Nuevo abeam.

The city of San Juan looks lovely from the sea. A mountainous background. The Capitol's white cupola shines in the morning sun. The old and large walls, buttresses, and gray towers of the ancient Spanish fortifications are in two distinct groups as seen from the sea. We passed the city at a distance of about 1 1/2 miles.

At 6:30 Point Porinquen, the N.W. corner of Puerto Rico, abeam. Course of 6:30 W.N.W.

Friday 7 July 1933. A fresh wind from east, but can carry all our canvas. Fast crossing of Morro Passage during the night. At 5:30 a.m. altered course to W. by N. Strong current. Some sea. Sighted land in S.W. at 9 a.m. but distant and not very distinct. It should be Cape Rafael, Haiti, or San Domingo. Speed around 6-6 1/2 miles.

A large shark 12-15 feet long has been zigzagging in our keelwater for a couple hours. A whale, a small one, light gray on the back and white on the belly, passed by us only a few fathoms away.

At noon Cape Samaná visible in S.W. At 4 p.m. Cape Cabrón abeam (S.S.W.). Wind very light E. We sailed in the 24 hours to noon today approximately 145 miles. Course W.N.W.

Cape Viejo Francés 18° 40' N. 70° W.

Saturday 8 July 1933. Wind fresh E. to E.N.E. At 3 a.m. we had Cape Viejo Francés abeam. At 7:30 a.m. we had Cape Macorís on a bearing S. and altered the course from W.N.W. to W. by N. At noon we had the bold and rocky promontory, Cape Isabela, abeam. Sailed from yesterday noon about 125 miles.

Visibility fair. A heat haze lays on the water and thickens over the land. No ships in sight. A lot of strange-looking seabirds about. In the afternoon the wind developed into a gale with rough sea. Keeping W.N.W. course to clear the 60-mile Montecristi Bank that at places has only four and five fathoms of water. Wind on the starboard quarter. Shortened sails.

Sunday 9 July 1933. Throughout the night the wind blew with gale force from the east. Hazy, but moonlight and no clouds. The sea was rough and very heavy, and continually breaking, making steering very difficult with the wind on the starboard quarter. Strong current. For 3 hours kept a N.W. course to make sure going clear of the Montecristi bank. Small sails throughout the night. At sunrise the wind moderated some and we altered the course to W.S.W. to get under land. At 7 a.m. had the eastern end of Tortuga Island (île de la Tortue) in S.S.E. Distant about 16 miles. Had passed Cape Haitien at midnight.

10 a.m. Still heavy sea but wind getting as usual again. All sails set. 10:30. Western end of Tortuga Island abeam. 3 p.m. Cape St. Nicholas, the northwestern end of Haiti, abeam (S.S.W.). Sea and wind have moderated and are as usual, but the latter

has veered to N.E. by E. Strong current setting S.W. Through the windward passage almost whole afternoon.

At 12 midnight we had Cape Maisí, the eastern extreme of Cuba, on a bearing south (Mag.) distant about 14 miles.

Monday 10 July 1933. Wind E. Smooth sea. Course W.N.W. At 6 a.m. had Point Guarico (Cuba) abeam. At 8 a.m. we were abreast of Moa Grande bay. At noon about due North of Point Tánamo, but steering well north to clear Point Lucrisia. Fresh east breeze. Passed a couple ships in the night north of Cape Maisí. We sailed to noon about 135 miles. Much seaweed, wood, and rubbish drifting in the current. At 7 p.m. we passed Lucrisia Point bearing south, distant 3 miles. At 9:30 we had Cape Samá abeam. At midnight we were about 12 miles from land and N.N.E. of Point Gibara. Cloudy and dismal-looking weather with a halo around the moon. Hope we won't run into a hurricane.

Tuesday 11 July 1933. Wind E. Course W.N.W. Smooth sea. 12 noon Port Manatí (Cuba) bearing S. At 4 o'clock in the afternoon Nuevitas light distant 5 miles was in S.W. (abeam). We altered the course to N.W. by N. for Lobos light and rigged our sails fore and aft again as the wind bore in almost abeam but on the starboard quarter a little yet.

The sea exceptionally smooth with a fine sail breeze. Some traffic, one ship going into Nuevitas, others going north our way through the Old Bahama channel. The land here is very low and the shoals and banks are treacherous, more so because a strong current is ever running N. (apparently). During the day, however, it is easy to see the shallows as they are invariably light green while deep water (edge) is always dark blue. And we draw only 2 feet 7 inches of water, so in a calm sea we can float over practically any shoal with a fathom of water on it. In a sea not by any means calm, over Horn Reef and Holt Knob (Amrum Bank), we did it and in the month of March, at the beginning of our voyage, with water ranging from one to 3 1/2 fathoms.

At 11 o'clock p.m. sighted Lobos Bay light (in N.N.W.). Wind dying down. Dark clouds and continuous lightning over Cuba (S. and S.W.).

Wednesday 12 July 1933. The air had a hurricane-like appearance last night and also today. Wind dying down and unsteady, changing around the compass-light and variable. Halo around the moon. Heavy squalls passing to the westward of us. Cirrus-like clouds and unbelievably hot and sultry air. We hove to from 12-3 a.m. Lobos Bay light abeam 9 a.m. Altered the course from N.W. by N. to W.N.W. for Paredon Grande Bay light.

Caught half a dozen dolphins this afternoon (2 to 2 1/2 feet long). They are a welcome change in our diet. Hope they'll taste O.K., and they no doubt will after our long diet of canned stuff.

6 p.m. Paredon Grande light abeam on a course of W.N.W Threatening black clouds to the S. and S.W. from which points a distant rumble of thunder reached our ears, and flashes of lightning are visible even now by daylight.

7:45 p.m. Very heavy squall. Thunder, lightning, green black clouds. Wind constantly changing. 10:15. In a dead calm N.N.W. of Paredon Grande light. Distant 10 miles.

Thursday 13 July 1933. Most of the night in a calm. At 6 a.m. got a light breeze from E.N.E. Caught a 3-foot-6-inch-long barracuda this morning. There are plenty of fish everywhere here.

Usual course of W.N.W. Nothing W. At 6 p.m. we had the light tower east of Bay Francés bearing S.W. 1/2 S. distant about 14 miles. The breeze has been rather dead today. Only 175 miles to Gary Reef light in Florida. Should make it in 40 hours if no squalls. Counting on the old Gulf Stream to push us along, too.

Friday 14 July 1933. S.E. breeze through the night, small, but enough to stiffen the canvas bunting and prevent slamming. At 12 midnight lost sight of the light E. of Francés Bay. It bore due S. (Mag) then. Variation here is only 2°. We altered the course from W.N.W. to N.W. by N. in mid-channel course. Through Santaren Channel. Some ships visible. A large quantity of seaweed floats about in the current. Today is extraordinarily hot and suffocating. A heat haze hangs over the sea.

At 1:15 p.m. sighted Anguilla Island on Cay Sal Bank in W. Probable distance away is 10 to 12 miles. Most of the afternoon the breeze was weak. Our little "TradeWind" moved ahead in it, although very slowly.

Saturday 15 July 1933. Light variable breezes and calm. Mostly from N.E. Course N.N.W. At 6:15 this morning we had the largest of the land islands on Damas Cays abeam. The current is not noticeable on the sea, but sets strongly in a N.W. direction. I calculated the distance from one of the keys to be around 6-7 miles, yet without any headway to speak of being made by sailing, a bearing taken after 45 minutes showed a difference of 3 1/2 points in the compass from the first bearing that was taken. During the forenoon the current set us greatly westward, but with close-hauled sheets we cleared the shore. The banks eastward of Damas Cays do not stretch as far E. and N.E. as indicated by the chart (U.S. 1411).

Seaweed in immense quantities floats about. Some of the accumulations are 100-150 feet in diameter. It is of the regular kind (Florida weed). The afternoon was squally with rain in torrents. At 4 o'clock in the afternoon we were abreast of the easternmost Dog Rocks. Wind and current forced us, however, to go to the west of the rocks. At 7 p.m. we had the westernmost of the rocks abeam. Course N.N.W.

We are certainly looking like a couple of hard cases now. Straggling, wild, unkempt long beards. Sunburned to an unbelievable dark color. Our glad rags are reaching an end now. We have used the clothes a lot, and a lot of clothes have spoiled or rotted away these months. But never mind. Smile, boy, smile. We'll probably walk up Broadway wrapped in blankets like regular old-time Siwashes. And the trip has been worth that and a lot, lot more. Something to remember in years to come.

Sunday 16 July 1933. Wind N.E. Course N.N.W. We are in the Gulf Stream. Some traffic. We have met 8-10 ships this morning.

Our provisions are getting scanty, but we have enough to last 12-15 days. Biscuits and flour, canned meats, onions, olive oil, and a little coffee and sugar. Also some of the dolphins we caught are in salt. Tobacco supply at low ebb and no tea to use instead, as when we rounded Cape Finisterre. But hope the wind is favorable. The current is. Should make New York in 10 days if everything goes well.

We are lying by the wind (12 noon) for close-hauled sheets on starboard tack. 4 p.m. We are beating N. on starboard tack and E. on port tack, trying to keep in the middle of the Gulf Stream. It sets north 3 and 3 1/2 knots (approximately 3 to 3 1/2 nautical miles per hour) here on the east coast of Florida. At 3 p.m. we sighted a lighthouse in N.W. that showed itself to be Fowey light to the south of Miami. At 5:45 p.m. we had it abeam. The city of Miami with its metropolitan-like skyline we had abreast (W.) at 7:40 p.m. We laid a course of N. and N. by E. with close-hauled sheets making a point leeway and drawing nearer and nearer to the coast that here runs in a N. by E. direction.

A large amount of traffic. The southbound close inshore. The northbound without exception well out (E.), barely visible.

After dark it was a wonderful sight for a shore-hungry sailor to see the brilliantly lighted skyscrapers and towers in the distant Miami.

Monday 17 July 1933. During the night the wind turned more E. so we could keep a course varying from N.N.E. to N.E. and so draw away from the shore without beating up to windward. At 4:20 a.m. we had passed Hillsboro and were abreast of Palm Beach. At 6:45 we had Jupiter light in W. Distant about 12-14 miles.

Florida! The Gulf Stream! These warm waters make life possible in its present form in Northern Europe. Its waters are here quite warm and I mean warm, not what we generally call warm water when going for a swim on a sunny summer day in Norway when the water really seems to be in the vicinity of an iceberg. Here the sea is really warm although the temperatures vary some.

From the Bay of Biscay we have followed this current—in a circle south of the coast of Spain and Portugal, to the Canaries, and across the Atlantic Ocean. Now the current flows N. and

E. all the way to the coast of Sunmøre, Lofoten, and Fin-marken—without us—giving life in these comparatively barren straits, in the form of an abundance of fish in the sea and a milder air, making vegetation possible. The air is noticeably chillier here at night than in the West Indies. In the afternoon it calmed down, a draft just enough to steer. But the current helps us along the right way—North.

(From Jupiter noon 50 miles.)

Tuesday 18 July 1933. Heavy rain squalls during the night. Passed some ships, mostly northbound but also a couple south-ward bound. At 8 o'clock this morning we were treated to a queer spectacle. A large waterspout about a mile and a quarter (or 1 1/2 miles) away. A black cloud hung overhead, but under the cloud no rain was falling or wind blowing. From the middle of this cloud an arm like the tentacle of an octopus shot down to the water. The sea was all aboil where this arm touched it, and an enormous amount of water was thrown up and described a circle before it fell again. And a lot of water was sucked up into the sky. The arm was blackish, so full of water it was, and I calculated the diameter of the arm to have been about 20-25 yards. The day is squally and hot with variable light breezes. Hope we can soon round Cape Hatteras.

At noon E. of Cape Canaveral. In about Latitude 28°30'N. (about). The nights are wonderful when steering this little nutshell "TradeWind." Stars overhead and clouds in phan-tomlike shapes and forms. The moon we have seen wax and wane four times. And one sits there on the homemade cushions with the back leaning against the compass top and thinks and dreams and sleeps in between when the weather is calm and the wind is sighing in the rigging. Or the white moon overhead and its silver beams on our snow-white sails.

Whatsoever happens in this, our little "TradeWind," this voyage I shall ever look back upon with the fondest memory. Its thrills and at times great dangers, and the tickling of the fancy at being called "Captain." Well, I have done the place-finding and have been at the head of this, so why not take the scanty and innocent honor there is in it? Life is worth living. Life is glorious. Only one thing is wonderful and God-like—life.

Course N. & E. (Noon 80 miles).

Wednesday 19 July 1933. Fine S.E. and S.S.E. breeze all night and to this forenoon. Course N. & E. Very strong current. Hundreds of porpoises frolicking about, some of them giving the boat a "smack" now and then. Some northbound traffic.

Sailing "deep water" and following a specified route. Viz— England, Spain, Portugal, Canary Islands, West Indies, Florida up to New York, without sextant, chronometer, barometer, log, and the other things—books, tables, which comprise a navigator's tools. It is not easy. It is not to take a chart only and lay a rule on it and "stick" up a compass from place to place. There is variation, deviation, leeway, and highly uneven and variable ocean currents. I did well across the North Sea. Made a mistake in the storms and adversity on the Bay of Biscay. Navigated perfect from Cape Roca to Anaga Rocks and from the Canary Islands to the West Indies. Was 50 miles off—N. (Anguilla). Easy to follow the coast up to Cape Florida, but a little more difficult from Jupiter to Cape Hatteras because of a very strong and shifting current. Yes, I have done remarkably well. Without boasting, may I say that. And the responsibility has rested on me, being the only "sailor" and the one having a working idea of navigation. (Noon 118 miles.) Course N.E. by N.

Considering we are in the latitude of Jacksonville and that the Gulf Stream hereabouts turns from a N. to a N.E. direction, I altered the course at noon to N.E. by N.

An immense quantity of fish has been seen today. Sharks, dolphins, flying fish, and many other kinds, the names of which I do not know. Squally, but sunshine in between.

Thursday 20 July 1933. Squally with heavy showers of rain. Variable light winds from S.E. to S.W., turning by S. All the way from Cape Florida the winds have been light and variable. Generally S. and S.S.W. in the daytime and after sundown to turn S.S.E. up to S.E.

Calculated to have made headway to noon 105 miles. Course N.E. by N. Visibility not very good, since the squalls are always obscuring some part of the horizon. In the latitude between 32°-33° N. Savannah—Cape Romain. In the afternoon we saw land far away in N.N.W. A Grace liner passed by us close this afternoon. Fresh wind turning W.S.W.

Friday 21 July 1933. Fresh S.W. breeze. Course N.E. by E. to 1 a.m., after which we altered it to E.N.E. to stand clear of light on Fryingpan Sh. which we had just sighted. At 7 a.m. we had it in N.N.W. High choppy sea. To noon about 120 miles.

Many sharks around the boat today. Had Paco's (Los Christianos) best cigar yesterday. It was my last tobacco and I enjoyed it more so because it was my last smoke for some time. Ah, how I love dame nicotine and absence (abstension) makes the heart grow fonder.

Variable very light winds, mostly from S.-S.W. this afternoon. In the latitude of Cape Fear 34°N., or between Cape Fear and Cape Lookout.

Saturday 22 July 1933. Light headwinds N. and N.E. Beating up N.E. under Cape Hatteras. Too far in to get real benefit from the Gulf Stream. On account of our provisions getting scanty, my partner is not very keen on following the stream, although it would take us along 60-80 miles a day. I would take a chance if alone, but since I have a partner I cannot take this responsibility if things went wrong. It would be worth a sporting shot, however.

East into the Gulf Stream. Stay in it till 150-200 miles N. of Cape Hatteras and cut across W. to Sandy Hook.

(Sailed to noon N.E. 35 miles.) Course N.E. to 6 a.m. From 6 a.m. N.N.W. At 6 p.m. we hailed "Lookout" Lightship outside Cape Lookout and got a supply of provisions and tobacco. How it tasted to get a real smoke again. Sailing E.S.E. for close-hauled sheets E. into the Gulf Stream.

Sunday 23 July 1933. Wind N.E. Course E. by N. In the strongest current with a good deal of northbound ships. Steering close by the wind for short sheets. Noon 45 miles sailed from "Lookout" Lightship. During afternoon varying courses E.N.E.

to N.E. Temperature of water 85° Fahrenheit.

One cannot help but smile at the Americans in the lightship which we visited yesterday. They remarked jokingly that we looked like Peary the time he returned from the North Pole. Presumably he had a wonderful crop of whiskers and hair as long as a middle-century Walter Raleigh that time. Well, I put my whiskers to the shears today. They were beginning to get in my way.

Lots of traffic N. and S. bound outside. Should be well abreast of Cape Hatteras this afternoon.

Outside Hatteras 35°7'N. 75°12'W.

23-7-33. H. M. Hamran.

Monday 24 July 1933. Course N.E. by N. Sailed to noon 50 miles. Current 50-100 miles N.E. Sea temperature 84° Fahr. Light variable winds N.W. to N. (Over N.)

Two southbound oil tankers. No life out here on the eastern edge of the main Gulf Stream. On the edge of it (the western) south of Cape Hatteras is the opposite. Sharks in schools up to a dozen can be seen, and not so small, either, generally 8-12 feet long. Also a large quantity of flying fish and plenty of dolphins. The last named are always chasing the winged ones, but without much success, apparently.

Day warm, but air refreshing. Course varying between N.N.E. and N. Cape Henry 37°N.76°W. Cape Charles 20 miles farther to the N. The two capes making the mouth or beginning of Chesapeake Bay. Cape Hinlopen to the south and Cape May to the north 17 miles distant (about) between the two, making the extreme forelands to Delaware Bay (Delaware River). Cape May lays in latitude 39°N. 75°W.

It would have been appropriate to arrive in New York on the 27th of this month, just four months after we departed from Kristiansand. It is two days to that date and less than 300 miles to Sandy Hook. Hope we will be able to make it. In afternoon could lay N.N.E. and N. Evening sea temperature 84° Fahr.

Tuesday 25 July 1933. Wind W. Good sail breeze through the night. Temperature of water fell in early morning hours from 84° to 78° around 8 a.m., to rise again to 80° Fahr.

Judging by this, we should be on the inside of the main Gulf Stream arm and fairly safe from being carried too far eastward in case we should fall into a calm. A few ships passed us on our west side going in a northerly direction.

Sailed to noon N.N.W. 110 miles. Noon almost calm with a little airing from S.S.W. Temperature of water (sea) at 6 p.m. 79° Fahr. Course N.N.W. A very hot day with a stifling thick atmosphere. Had the last of Stumpf's beef carbonades for dinner. They were good to the last.

An English ship, the "Baron Kelvin," passed by close this afternoon going north. Everybody was on deck waving in greeting to us. They probably have read about us in the English newspapers or heard of us in St. Thomas, Virgin Islands.

Wednesday 26 July 1933. Calm through the night with light airings and breezes from all directions. Inky-black-violet cloud banks on the horizon both in S.W. and in the early morning hours in S.E., with a profusion of lightning and an almost continuous rumble of thunder, but we did not get into any rain squalls. Temperature of sea 75° Fahr.

Some ships southbound. Kept an average course of N.W. Sailed to noon about 45 miles. Current uncertain. Calculate we are in the latitude of Cape May and not far from the coastline.

At 2 p.m. the "Minnesotan" of the American Hawaiian Line came 2-3 miles off her course and asked us if we were all right and where we were bound for and came from. Someone has perhaps reported us in New York, or what's more probable, they thought we were a fishing smack from the coast and had drifted out to sea and needed assistance. Seamanly and sportingly done, anyway, in any case. 8 p.m. Fresh wind N.E.

Thursday 27 July 1933. Gale from E.N.E. At 2 a.m. took in the jib. At 3 a.m. reefed the mainsail. At 5:30 in the morning we lay a course of N.N.E. for staysail and double-reefed mainsail. Even so, she had more than she could carry. Rain squalls and crosswise choppy seas that continually broke over us. We are leaking a good deal. Cape May abeam at 6 a.m. During forenoon the weather moderated some and the sea lay down some. Both of us up through the night on account of the leak.

At 12 noon calm. N.W. of "Five Fathoms" Lightship and half-way between it and Cape May. Only 100 miles to New York, but oh, how hard to make it in this weather!

Friday 28 July 1933. Calm with light airings from the south and S.W. On the coast of New Jersey. At noon we had Atlantic City abreast (W). Steering a course of N.E. by N.

A large amount of traffic N. and S. Similar to that usually found in the Strait of Dover. It is a wonderful day—sunshine and pleasantly cool. In the distance, about 8 miles off, is the metropolitan-like skyline of Atlantic City, the playground by the sea for the cooped-up populations of the large cities by the bays and inlets on the N.E. Atlantic coast.

Viewed from the sea, Atlantic City has a dozen skycrapers, and as the landscape here is low and very flat, the buildings and towers appear large and unreal.

Well, we have battled and tracked our way through 7,000 miles of the waters of the different shores of the Atlantic Ocean and now have only 70 or 80 miles left of our route with New York as our destination—12 hours with good sailing but with this weather a couple of days. But it may change anytime and it probably will. We are sailing along with the Norwegian flag at the masthead and are doubtless creating no small amount of curiosity on the ships and pleasure fishing boats that pass by us.

6:45 p.m. Passed "Barnegat" Lightship off 2 miles. Fresh S.S.W. At 10 p.m. we sighted Sandy Hook light and had it abeam (W.) at 12 o'clock. Thousands of lights on the shoreline and bright in the sky over Manhattan Island.

Deck Cleat

New York at last!

What Harald Hamran described as "our little TradeWind"
looks rather large to some Vesterheim visitors.

Welcome to New York

Saturday 29 July 1933. Calm from midnight to 4:30 a.m. A little breeze then rose from W. and with close-hauled sheets we kept close and hugged the shore of the sand key that goes in a northerly direction from Sandy Hook. Visibility poor. Course N.W. by N. Saw the lightship for a moment in E.N.E. through the haze. Distant about 5 miles. Many fishing smacks.

At 8:15 a.m. we rounded the north point on the Sand Key with the lighthouse. At the quarantine station 12 noon; everything O.K. Towed by a Government tug to the foot of 69th Street Brooklyn.

Many reporters. Many photographers. Many visitors, men and women of all classes, and hundreds of girls. Mostly Scandinavians, but also a lot of Americans and other nationalities. Dinner with a Norwegian captain's family (Gundersen). To bed at 2:30 and even then there were half a dozen girls sitting up on the quayside. A great day and "terra firma" at last. It is good to be ashore.

Sunday 30 July 1933. Had a fine night's rest aboard. For different reasons, we did not shift ashore when we arrived here. Everything is undecided yet. We may go up to the Chicago Fair if suitable arrangements can be made. Visitors from early morning on the wharf. Some of them come right on us and even kiss us—women, of course. Vang studio made 106 postcards of our boat and they sold here on the wharf in half an hour, our friends here in Brooklyn doing the selling. Getting some more tomorrow.

Dinner invitations to go everywhere. People are extraordinarily nice, and take an unbelievable interest in us and our boat. And a lot of girls and women, almost French in their attention and interest. All the New York papers had articles about us and pictures of our "TradeWind."

This is the end of a perfect day. Have invitations to stay ashore with private families and also in the "Norwegian-American Republican Club."

Monday 31 July 1933. After a good night's rest we went ashore and cleared our papers of arrival with the customs house.

Received some remuneration from *Nordisk Tidende* for the articles that have been written during the voyage. Sold 144 photos of the boat in half an hour. $(144 + 106$ yesterday $= 250)$.

Thousands of visitors and invitations to go here and there. Gundersen, the Norse-American Republican League, to Captain Charles Crownshield, to Strømstedt, to Olsen Towing Co., to Captain Magnus Anderson.

And such a lot of girls. And they are as nice and as entertaining and good-looking as only American and especially Brooklyn girls can be. And they want to know all about the trip and a lot about ourselves. So there are a lot of questions to answer. And one does not mind answering questions—even try to make the answers as long and complicated as possible—when the questioner is young and slim and good-looking.

Tuesday 1 August 1933. "Fox Films" wishes to film us with Magnus Anderson tomorrow. Gave Vang studios an order for 500 photos. Getting another 500 printed (1,000). Many visitors.

Nordisk Tidende has a large piece about our voyage and ourselves. Everything is deliriously grand and exciting.

Disposed of 120 photos. Had dinner at Christiansens. Thousands of visitors to see the "TradeWind" and us, and hundreds of girls.

Wednesday 2 August 1933. Fox Films (newsreels) photographed us and the boat as "news" this forenoon. Guests at the Norse Club for lunch. Dinner at Strømstedt. Many visitors. Disposed of about 150 photos.

Thursday 3 August 1933. Usual lot of visitors. Sold out our photos. Refused to go to Viking Bar as it seems to be a place with a bad reputation. These are busy, pleasant, and hectic days. Hundreds of people to see us every day, and some are very nice and very interesting. Invitations everywhere, but have no time to accept these.

Visit of Captain Magnus Anderson this evening. Representatives from different clubs have been here today.

Some mail from home. The girls are very enthusiastic about us and do not know what they can do for us.

Kristiansand, S. Mandal, Farsund, Flekkefjord, Oslo, and other nationalities: French, English, Swedish, American, Ruth Oldman. What a glorious life. *Deilige mat—Deilige jord* (Delicious food—Beautiful world).

Friday 4 August 1933. Same as other days, busy refusing invitations. Have decided to leave for Chicago on Tuesday or Wednesday next week. Everything is going our way except the money part of it, which could have been better. The ladies are much interested in us and have shown it in many ways.

"TradeWind" Harald Hamran

Saturday 5 August 1933. Very busy. To a reception in the Norse Republican League. Gave a short lecture.   H.H.

Sunday 6 August 1933. Thousands of visitors, but we appreciated most the visit of Magnhild Hansen Fjellheim. To a little reception in the North of Norway Association, where I made a little speech about the trip. Getting used to terra firma again. Maybe towing can be arranged right from here in New York to Lake Erie.

Monday 7 August 1933. Had invitations from some private people to come to their homes, and the Norwegian Seamen's Church shall today send out invitations for a party in our honor on Thursday night.

Lawrence Wilson, Bjørnson, and Victor Dujo have arranged for us to go up Broadway and be received by the mayor of New York—O'Brien.

Thousands of visitors. This evening to a reception in the Norwegian League *(Den Norske Nationaflorbund)*. In Nelson's home for dinner.

Towing through the Erie Canal can probably be arranged for us by Olsen, Nelson, and Håkonsen. The days are busy and life is rather sweet in all this enthusiasm and interest people are showing in our venture. The women and girls have been especially nice to us here in Brooklyn.

Tuesday 8 August 1933. Usual people. Receptions in New York arranged. *Nordisk Tidende* has a good deal to say about our stay in New York. To visit Hanna Arntzen. Had a large sign made for the boat. Smith gave us some rope and stuff.

Brooklyn, New York

Wednesday 9 August 1933. At 9 in the morning we shifted away from the 69th Street pier and over to the Battery Park. At 11 a.m. we started the procession up Broadway to the City Hall, where we were received by a representative of the city of New York. Our friends from South Brooklyn had turned up in numbers and were very enthusiastic. In the parade up Broadway were Mr. W. Morgenstierne, Consul General, Mr. Singstad, the architect, Arnesen from *Nordisk Tidende,* Solberg, Slytander, Brekke, and representatives from Norse organizations in Brooklyn.

In the evening we shifted back to the 69th Street pier and had the usual crowd of curious visitors with us. Lunch in the Norse American Republican League.

New York, 9 August 1933.

Thursday 10 August 1933. Usual crowd, maybe a little less than usual. Presented to and greeted by Hasselberg, the Borough president of Brooklyn, and later to lunch in the Elliott Club. Shown around Brooklyn by Arnesen and Hansen. In the Norwegian Seamen's Church in the evening. Taken home by Christiansen and Halvorsen. Provisions sent down by Alfred Anderssen. A busy and fine day.

Brooklyn, New York, 10 August 1933.

Friday 11 August, 1933. Rainy. The only day we have not had many visitors. Rung up the Olsen Towing Co. and at 2:30 p.m. the "John G. Olsen," a large tugboat, came to the 69th Street pier and took us past lower Manhattan up the North river, where we tied up to a barge. Will get upriver tonight.

It was certainly a hurry-up good-bye to our friends on the pier there at 69th Street, as we had only a few minutes to cast loose from the pier and get hold of the towing line from our tug. Good-bye Brooklyn and New York. Good-bye Bay Ridge. I am leaving you with regrets and I have only the best—yes, unforgettable—memories of you and the people's welcome to us there. So *au revoir*, we have to keep our word and go farther.

On to Chicago.

Cooking and sleeping were below deck. Hamran brothers got there through this cabin hatch.

73

Onward to Chicago

Saturday 12 August 1933. At 12:30 a.m. we hurry onto a tug with some barges going up the Hudson. The day nice and sunny. Boats going upstream and boats going downstream wave and greet us. As everywhere else, they are surprised at seeing this little Lister boat flying the Norwegian flag and no doubt they wonder what it is all about.

Brooklyn—what a nice time you gave us. Parties and feasts in our honor, and perhaps what we like to remember more than anything else—the thousands of interesting visitors on the pier. The warm balmy, half-dark August evenings and the nice girls who wanted to know such a lot about us and our voyage.

"Man skal se mere på æren en på et langt liv" (one should look more on the honor than on a long life).

Sunday 13 August 1933. Hanging onto a tow. Very slow. Boats going up and coming down river hail us and we are naturally of interest to the people on both sides of the river.

It is very interesting to go up this river. Past the world-famous "Sing Sing" penitentiary, under gigantic bridges, past the residences of the Vanderbilts, Astors, and Roosevelts.

Not for nothing is the Hudson River named "The American Rhine." To go up this river these August evenings is like being on a vacation. It is great to live, to be sound, to see, and to understand in this glorious green beautiful world.

On the Hudson River. Harald Hamran

Monday 14 August 1933. Passed in the early morning hours through Albany and Troy. Reports from Albany newspaper. We are in Waterford, waiting for a chance to get farther up the Erie Canal. Some visitors hanging around. Around noon a tug passing up with an oil barge was willing to take us in tow.

The country here is wonderful. Small summer camps and summer houses. Canoes and small speedboats in the canal, where in places it takes on the characteristics of a lake. Sun-

74

shine and wind, and many pretty women. We passed through 6 locks in the early afternoon. All in all, there are 35 of these between Troy and Buffalo.

Tuesday 15 August 1933. Awake all through the night, and minding the boat in the locks. There are more than 300 bridges spanning this Erie Canal, and as mentioned before 35 locks. Night chilly and raw with some fog! Our towing with the "Margaret Ronan" came to an end at Fort Plain, but immediately we picked up another (the state of New York tug "Dewitt Clinton"). That took us as far as Lock 17. Hung on the Shell barge, the L.T.C. No. 2, to Illion, where we tied up for the night.

On the Erie Canal. H. M. Hamran

Wednesday 16 August 1933. Departed Illion 6 a.m. with our Shell barge from yesterday. It is going to Syracuse, so we'll have come a good way when it leaves us.

At Lock 20 a lady reporter from a Utica newspaper got some news from me about the voyage. A cameraman took some pictures.

Today is a fine day. Sunshine and refreshingly cool air. People in passing cars and pedestrians and loafers on the canal banks are waving to us.

We have a sign on a billboard 6x4 feet on the deck. On it is painted: "By Sail from Kristiansand to Chicago," our names, the size of our boat, when we left Norway, and when we arrived in New York. It is amusing to see some people running to a place just to read the sign. It is painted only on one side.

In the afternoon we arrived at Sylvan Beach, where the canal from east runs into Lake Oneida. Many bathers and many in the summer camp. Some speedboats follow us, coming alongside to read the billboard (Lovely Lady). Lake Oneida is a dream of beauty.

In the evening we parted company with our tug (barge) the L.T.C. No. 2, Wilmington, Delaware, and tied up inside of Lock 23. 200 miles from Buffalo.

Thursday 17 August 1933. Caught onto a slow drag at 3:30 a.m. Slow but better than laying moored.

Passing many summer camps on the canal banks. Our little Norwegian flag *"Smeld i vind"* (flutters in the wind) on our highest place aboard—the lowered mast. Under and among the green trees the Stars and Stripes fly above the camps and occasionally entwine themselves among the green leaves and branches of the trees. One can almost forget all troubles in this beauty.

Many good-looking and some beautiful mermaids in bathing costumes, some in the water swimming, others on the canal banks, have been hired as cooks and stewardesses and handy-men (women). Others in pleasure boats passing us, or in canoes, ask a couple questions and wave us a friendly greeting.

I have heard and read many things about the U.S. and its people, and mostly adverse criticism. But I have found a friendly and natural and energetic and clean people, far ahead of any other that I in my capacity have ever dreamed to know.

The average American is good-humored, optimistic, energetic, sociable in a free, unconventional manner, frank and open, very generous, always a gambler, and he looks on the rest of the world as inferior. In a way he is right. He is on the average better housed, better fed, better paid, and can buy books and have amusements and recreation of a kind denied to his caste elsewhere in the world—radio, automobile, newspapers, have a summer camp for the weekend, see moving pictures, and many other things in this class.

Friday18 August 1933. Hanging behind our tug from yesterday, coming out of Lock 28B, was a boat with a large crowd aboard. An American youth, talking through a megaphone, shouted: "We wish you luck; we admire your pluck," after which the entire crowd gave us a ringing "Hurrah."

The usual crowd of curious visitors at the locks and on the bridges and on the canal banks. Passed through Lock 29, Palmyra, at 6 p.m. We are 117 miles from Buffalo.

Saturday 19 August 1933. Fine weather. Sunshine and W. breeze. At 6 a.m. we passed Rochester. At the locks at night there are always some curious onlookers. Apropos locks: We have passed 33 and have only two left. Thank God!

On our way through this Erie Canal I have hired God knows how many cooks, stewardesses, able seamen (or women) mates and just companions for the next crossing of the Atlantic. A couple hundred at least—some in bathing suits, some young and pretty, and some white-haired and motherly. I have certainly got my hands full for the next 25-30 years.

Seriously, we appreciate the interest people take in us and the "TradeWind."

Sunday 20 August 1933. Nearing our first stop, Buffalo. 10 a.m. 40 miles. Amusing to listen to the conversation among the groups on the bridges we pass under:

1. "Across in that thing? Well, I'll be damned."
2. "You sure must have courage."
3. "You must have pluck. We wish you all kinds of luck."
4. "Is that the boat that came from Norway?"
5. "I wish I was a boy" (man)—from women.

At 2 p.m. we arrived at Lockport and passed through the last two locks in the canal—34 and 35.

People in the cars passing over the bridges and speeding along the roads by the canal are waving to us and want to know how we like this part of the U.S. Since we came to the U.S., up to now, I have not heard an unfriendly or unkind word said to us.

At Lockport there were about 200-250 curious onlookers and of course the usual number of questions. Telephone call from Chamber of Commerce Buffalo in care of Lockkeeper-Lockport.

Monday 21 August 1933. A strong current makes progress slow. We are now about 6 miles from Buffalo (10 a.m.) and making 1/2 mile per hour.

On our arrival in Buffalo we tied up at the motor boat club and in a short time the place was crowded with reporters and newspaper photographers. The Norwegian consul, Mr. Munch-Kielland, came aboard and wished us welcome. (Mr. Hagen and wife.)

I went over to the Coast Guard station and tried to see the captain on the matter of arranging a tow across Lake Erie. Nothing decided so far.

In the evening a guest at the motor boat club.

Buffalo, 21 August 1933   Harald Hamran

Tuesday 22 August 1933. The Buffalo press is making a headline of our voyage. Large pictures and the same old story about our crossing. (Dorothy Wilson.)

At 10:30 a.m. with the Norwegian Consul as guide and introducer, we left on a sight-seeing round of Buffalo, and paid our respects to some prominent Buffalo citizens: Mr. Hagen, Mr. Rasmussen of the Coast Guard, Mr. Boland and Cornelius, which latter is arranging for our trip to Chicago. Also at the Chamber of Commerce and some other places. Very interesting. In the afternoon a large crowd visited us. Like New York only on a smaller scale.

We are leaving for Milwaukee Friday.   Many Norwegians among the visitors, also Swedish and Danish. People are very hospitable. The end of a perfect day.

Buffalo, 22-8-33.

Wednesday 23 August 1933. Many visitors, among them many girls and women. Commander Martin Rasmussen of the Coast Guard was here most of the forenoon. Dinner at 5:30 with Mr. Hagen and wife and Mr. Kielland. Very interesting and enjoyable. Some very nice women to see us in the afternoon. Made honorary members of the Motorboat Club of Buffalo. The club has been very hospitable to us.

At times, Hans is maybe more in the limelight than I. But I don't mind it. His experience at sea is a matter of 8 years while mine is 20-22. I am the man behind it all with plans, and it rests with me in all things.

Late in the evening we had a visit of a family Haddock and a girl, Helen Snell, one of the prettiest women I have ever seen. Dorothy Wilson came to see me.

There is a storm warning. Storm here at 12:30 a.m.

Buffalo, New York, 23 August 1933. Harold Magnus Hamran

Thursday 24 August 1933. Rainy and blowing, but we are well-sheltered here in the basin. At 9 a.m. we got orders from Boland and Cornelius and a floating crane came from the drydock and lifted us on deck. We got across the harbor and alongside the "Harry Yates," which is going to take us to Milwaukee. We dumped the sand, 700 pounds of it, which was taken aboard as ballast in Kristiansand in March.

I like the sea, but a little rest ashore would be welcome now. Since we left Kristiansand, we have had little time, and spend 3 to 4 days in port writing and clearing the papers, leaving and arriving.

At 3:15 this afternoon the boat was hoisted by the drydock crane and put on a hatch on the "Harry Yates." Here aboard they all seem to be good sportsmen and we may be satisfied with the whole transaction. Rain and miserable weather.

Summary

From Kristiansand to Dover	550
Dover-St. Vincent (Portugal)	1,105
St. Vincent-Anaga Rocks	720
Anaga Rocks-Los Christianos	60
Teneriffe-Anguilla	2,760
Anguilla-Bay Rock	1,100
Bay Rock-Jupiter	205
Jupiter-Sandy Hook	930
Miles - Straight Line	7,362
Miles - sailed	8,302 miles
	Harald Hamran

In the evening we were visited by several families connected with Boland and Cornelius office staffs. In the salon of the "Harry Yates" we gave an outline of the trip, and the girls and women were very much interested in it.

This book is a logbook and diary from March 1933 to August 1933 of the preparations and the trip from Norway to the United States and as far as Buffalo, New York.

Buffalo, New York, 24 August 1933. Harald Magnus Hamran

Waterspout as drawn by Harald M. Hamran
in his log-diary, July 18, 1933

Editor's note: The brothers' crossing of the ocean under sail ended at New York City. The "TradeWind" was towed to Buffalo, was hoisted aboard another ship to Milwaukee, and proceeded under sail to Chicago, Illinois, where the brothers were welcomed and attended the Chicago World's Fair. The last entry in this log/diary was made in Buffalo.

In 1934, Harald Hamran attempted to cross the Atlantic solo in a tiny boat, and was lost at sea. Hans Hamran returned to Norway and built a home which he called "Enebo" (hermit's dwelling) in the valley of the Vidala river near Hedalen, Valdres. He died in 1971.